HARDPRESS.NET
HOME OF HARD-TO-FIND BOOKS

Little Rosy's Travels: Or, Country Scences in the South of France
by Rosy (Little, Fict.Name.)

Address:
HardPress
8345 NW 66TH ST #2561
MIAMI FL 33166-2626
USA
Email: info@hardpress.net

Little Rosy's travels

Pierre Jules Hetzel

'Rosy thought she might as well pack her own box, and save her Mamma the trouble. Dear Mamma would be so pleased.'

LITTLE R... TRAVELS

COUNTRY SC... ... ...

...

Second ...

... JACKSON, AND HALLIDAY, ...
LON... M.CCC.XVII...

LITTLE ROSY'S TRAVELS:

OR,

COUNTRY SCENES IN THE SOUTH OF FRANCE.

With Twenty-four Illustrations by L. Frölich.

Second Edition.

SEELEY, JACKSON, AND HALLIDAY, FLEET STREET.
LONDON. MDCCCLXVIII.

CONTENTS.

Contents.

LITTLE ROSY'S TRAVELS.

CHAPTER I.

PACKING UP.

THE summer had come and gone, and the autumn had come too and was nearly gone, when Rosy Girard sat on her papa's knee one evening and heard a grand piece of news. None of my little friends could ever guess what this piece of news was about; or what made her clap her little fat hands so very loud, and give her dear papa so many hugs and kisses: so they may

B

as well be told at once that Rosy was going into the country, and that was the very thing she liked above all things.

Now Rosy had been born in London, and every day when it was fine she went out, of course, like other little girls, for what nurse called 'a nice walk in one of the squares.' She had no little brother or sister to go with her; but then she had her dear doll, Julia, who always went out with her, and to whom she told all her secrets. Sometimes, too, she took her hoop, and had great games with that while nurse carried Miss Julia for her. Still, though Rosy liked these walks all very well, they were nothing like such good fun as it would be to run about in the sweet fields, picking flowers, and making daisy-chains for her dear mamma; or playing on the sea-shore with the sand

and shells, while the wild waves 'ran after her.'

Rosy was going a very long way off, first in a train, and then in a boat, and then in a train again, till she came to a place where it would be warm all the winter, and where she would be able to pick flowers just when her little cousins in England were making snow-balls. In short, Rosy was going to a place called Cannes in her papa's own country, France. For Rosy's mamma had been very poorly lately, and papa was sure there was no place like that for making her strong again.

It was a fine thing to tell nurse certainly, —or rather to make nurse guess. Rosy thought she never could guess it right; but somehow she did, even to the day when they were to go; and when she had washed the little girl and put on her night-gown, the good nurse bid her kneel down by her little bed and pray to her great Father in heaven that He would take care of them all on that long, long journey, and make the nice, warm place do dear mamma a great deal of good, so that she might come back quite strong and well again. Afterwards she gave Rosy a kiss and tucked her up very tight and snug in bed, and told her to go to sleep very fast because they were going to begin packing to-morrow.

Rosy wished very much then that to-morrow were already come; but her little eyelids soon shut over the blue eyes and did not open again until it was nearly breakfast time.

How busy the little maiden was all that morning! First she had to dress Julia, of course; and while she was putting her day clothes on, she had to tell her the good news.

Rosy fancied, however, that the good doll was not much pleased; she said that she had made a great face when she heard that she was going away from all the fine shops; but that might have been fancy, of course. Dolls are never so rude as to make faces !

Rosy's mamma and nurse were very busy packing up all day; and they went out two or three times to buy things which they thought would be wanted for the journey; so the little girl was left to run about, and amuse herself with her doll; but she did not like to see other people busy, and do nothing but play herself; so she thought she might as well pack her own box, and save her mamma the trouble. Dear mamma would be so pleased when she found it was all done, and that she had not got to stoop down any more.

First, she put in the dearest of all her treasures, I mean Julia herself, her cradle, and all the dolly's clothes, the common ones, and the company frocks, the beautiful new hat, and the two cloaks, as well as the shoes and stockings.

Next came a cage with another great pet, Mr. Tommy, the yellow canary which Uncle Henry had given her not long ago. This cage was on the nursery table, as it happened that day, and the little girl managed very cleverly, as she thought, by mounting on a chair to draw it to the edge; and then when she got down again she was just able to carry it in her little fat hands from the table to the box, though in doing so she spilt some of the water in the glass and made the cage very wet.

It was a great matter to get Julia and Tommy safely packed, and Rosy thought she was getting on splendidly. But there were two other treasures that must go too; and these were a beautiful vase of flowers which grandmamma had given her only yesterday, and the rose-tree which still had many roses on it, and from which Rosy often picked one as a present for mamma.

The vase got quite safely into its corner, and the great big pot was tightly clasped in the fat round arms, and just going to be popped in. It was almost too heavy for the little woman to carry; and perhaps in going down into its place the hard pot might have broken the glass vase. Mamma, however, came into the room just in time.

She showed her little girl that the lid of the trunk could never shut over so tall a thing; how dark it would be for the poor bird if he were fastened up for so long a time; and besides that, if all these things went in, there would be no place for Rosy's own frocks and pinafores. So, though it did cost a few tears at first when she thought of leaving the dickey-bird and the flowers behind, yet the little maiden was very brave and choked down her sobs as soon as she could, that she might go with a pleasant face to ask dear grandmamma to take care of her treasures until she came back again to Old England.

Grandmamma lived just across the road;

but nurse was so very busy that Rosy had to coax Sally the housemaid to tie on her hat and take her over. She could not be quite happy again until she knew that dear little Tommy would have some one to sing to, and some one to give him seed and water every morning. But when the good grandmamma had promised to take great care of him, and to water the rose-tree every day, she came back very fast that the good-natured Sally might have time to run back with them both before dinner-time.

And then when Rosy had said good-bye two or three times to Tommy, and picked one pretty rose for mamma's waistband, she ran into the nursery, and was soon very busy again folding up her doll's clothes and putting them into a little box

which her mamma had given her on purpose.

So Rosy had some packing to do after
all.

CHAPTER II.

IN THE TRAIN.

THE happy 'journey-day' soon came, and Rosy found herself for the first time looking out of the window of a train. At first the loud whistles and shrieks of the engine made her just a little bit afraid as she walked along the platform; and she held her papa's hand very tightly. But when they got into the carriage he took her on his knee and told her that it was only in a hurry to be off, so she tried to laugh, and very soon they began to move, and every thing seemed to move too.

'Oh, look, papa,' she said, 'all the houses are running along, and the bridges too; look, they are running away from us so fast!'

It was a long while before she could understand that the houses and bridges stood just where they always had done, and that the train with Rosy in it was running away from them.

They seemed to go over the tops of a great many houses, and passed some very narrow streets. And down a long way below them, on the pavements and in the roads, there were many children at play. But they were poor, ragged children, with pale faces, and they did not look happy at all.

Rosy saw some also looking out of the windows with their mothers, and she turned

'Oh, look, Papa, all the houses are running along! and the
bridges, too!'

round and said to her mamma that they were dirty and cross, not nice little girls at all.

'And how would Rosy look,' asked mamma, 'if she had had no breakfast this morning, or if nurse were ill and could not wash her face, or if she were very ill herself, and no one had money to buy her medicine?'

Rosy looked very grave then, and said she would save some of her pennies to give these poor little children when she came back again; and by that time they had passed the narrow streets and had come to some very, very large houses with great, tall chimneys; and papa told her that once upon a time he had been inside a place like those, and seen lots of boys and girls helping to make the little round night-lights, one of which nurse once had burning all night in a saucer when Rosy was sick.

Afterwards they passed some very bare fields with little rows of cabbages growing first here and there in patches, and a few very black-looking trees; and the little girl cried out so loud that they were coming to the country at last, that she quite startled an old gentleman, who was trying to go to sleep in the opposite corner, and made papa say,——

'Hush, Rosy! not so loud; we shall see something much prettier soon.'

And so they did. For in a little while out of both windows they could only see real green fields and delightful hills, with many trees growing on them. And Rosy, who was beginning to grow tired of sitting still, thought she should very much like to get out for a little while and pick daisies and buttercups.

So mamma looked in her bag to find a biscuit, and told Rosy that when she had eaten that she had better go to sleep.

Papa put some carpet-bags for mamma to rest her feet upon, and he put his little girl down by her side; and though she was quite sure that she was not one wee bit sleepy, yet mamma soon saw the little head begin to droop and the eyelashes fall over the eyes; and then she just put her arm round her darling, and both of them went fast asleep.

They were waked up again by a very loud squeal from the engine, and by feeling that the train was stopping.

Rosy started up, and was so frightened that she began to cry. But her kind papa took her in his arms again, and said ' it was all right; they were only stopping at a station.' And though Rosy did not know what they meant, yet she saw that there was a great bustle, and that some people were getting out and others getting in to the carriages.

She asked whether it were not time for them to get out too; but mamma said,—

'Oh no, dear, not yet; you had better lie down and go to sleep again.'

But Rosy was wide awake now, and besides just at that moment there came up to the carriage door a very merry-looking little boy, with a monkey on his shoulder. The monkey had a chain fastened to his leg and looked very good-tempered, though rather mischievous; and the boy wanted to get into the carriage and bring his monkey too.

Rosy's mamma looked rather frightened about this, and papa said it could not come in. He told its young master to have it put with the dogs, or anywhere, except among the passengers; but Rosy said,—

'Oh, do let it come in, papa! It will be such fun.'

Just then up came a man to take the monkey away; and Rosy looked quite disappointed till her papa told her that monkeys are often very spiteful, and will bite and scratch.

Then she thought she would rather not have such a companion, though she did want something to play with very badly. And to her great joy, just before the train started again, in came an old lady with a little girl just about her own size, and a large bird-cage covered with a shawl.

Oh, how curious she was to know what sort of bird was under that shawl! But she had not to wait long; for very soon the other little girl began to pull it aside, and Rosy heard something say,—

'Pretty Polly! pretty Polly! pretty dear.'

'Oh, mamma, a parrot, I do declare!' said Rosy, in a very loud whisper, as she slid down off the seat, and, with her finger in her mouth, sidled up to the cage.

Rosy was rather bashful sometimes, but she soon got over it now, when the kind old lady asked her to come and look at her little one's pet.

It was a beautiful green bird, with a long tail, and a rose-coloured ring round its neck, and it seemed to like little girls very much, and came to the front of the cage to talk to them.

Her papa told Rosy that the parrot and the monkey most likely came from the same country,—a country where it was too hot for little girls to go out in the middle of the day. And the old lady said that her little girl had only just come from that hot country, and that it was called India She said, too, that Polly came with her and could say her name, which was Annie; and she put the two little girls side by side and told them to be very good friends, and talk to each other until they got to Dover.

So Rosy had a great pleasure on that first train-journey of hers, and she and Annie played very nicely together without quarrelling at all until they were not far from their journey's end.

Then Rosy went back to her mamma and said she was tired of playing. So papa

lifted her on his knee again, and let her
look out of the window and watch for Dover
Castle, and the first peep of the sea and the
ships.

CHAPTER III.

STILL ON THE JOURNEY.

BUT still the train went on and on. Now there was a whistle just as if it were going to stop, and Rosy strained her eyes to see what they were coming to, and strained them in vain. At last she said she was quite sure that ' Dover was never coming at all,' and quietly laid her head against her papa and began to amuse herself with his watch and seals. And what do our little readers think happened then? Why then, in spite of her having made up her mind *not* to go to sleep, she *did* go to sleep. And when mamma saw that she said ' it was a very good thing.'

So papa did not wake her up, but held her tight and snug. His arm made a very comfortable pillow, and for a counterpane he put a shawl over her.

The train went jogging and shaking on, till it rocked her into a sounder sleep than I think she had ever had in her life. And then, as most people do, Rosy began to dream.

Dreams are sometimes very nasty things, and sometimes very nice ones, you know. Sometimes when little boys and girls have been dreaming they wake up laughing; that must be when the dream was about something funny; sometimes they wake up crying, and that must be when the dream was about ,omething which they do not like.

Well, Rosy's dream was rather a nice one, and rather a long one too; and it was partly about something that she liked very much indeed. I mean her dear dolly, who was all this while lying comfortably in the trunk that Rosy had helped to pack.

In her dream Rosy forgot all about this journey, and thought that she was in the Zoological Gardens, carrying Julia in one arm, and a bun for the bears in the other hand.

It was a large bun, and Rosy could not help thinking that there would be enough left for the bears if she were to take just a little bite herself. But then her mamma told her that it was not the sort of bun that she would like, that it had a bitter taste. So, in her dream, Rosy hoped that when she got home again her dear mamma might perhaps give her a nice piece of cake instead if she were very good.

So she walked on very fast and talked to Julia as she went along. She told her that bears bite, and even eat little children if they can get them, and that they growl and fight, and that little children must not be like bears.

Rosy thought that it was very hot in these gardens, and that she ran on the grass, and wished she might pick some flowers. But the grass was not thick and soft under her feet, but brown and dry, and in some places it was all trodden off.

There seemed to be a great many people walking along, and the bears' den seemed to be just in front of them, yet though they all kept walking on no one seemed to get near it.

Rosy thought too that she saw the pelicans, and all the curious water-birds only a little way off, some in their cages, some by the water side. She heard the monkeys, and peeped in at the door of the great monkey-house. But that was full of people too. She only saw two monkeys high up in their cage, grinning at one another; and one of these monkeys had got a sort of paper cap which he would keep squeezing on to the head of the other monkey, over face and all, so that he could not see a bit. And when Rosy saw that, she told Julia that that was mischief, and that *she* must not be mischievous.

Then they seemed to go on again, and to come to the lions' den, where the lions and lionesses were walking up and down, just as they always do, looking at the people

now and then, but not at all unkindly. And
Rosy told Julia that ' the lion was the king
of beasts,—papa said so.'

All this was in her dream, you know.
She did not really see anything, though in
the summer time she had been to these gardens with her papa and mamma, and now
in her sleep she thought she was there again.

It seemed to be a long time that she
wandered about, seeing all kinds of animals
and birds, but never getting any nearer to
the bears the whole time.

And all the while she thought that she
was talking to her doll, and teaching her to
be good. How very odd it is that little girls
always know exactly how dolls ought to
behave, and so often forget to be good
themselves!

Rosy finished her dream by thinking

that she and Julia went home in a goat-chaise. She thought that she had the reins in her own hand, and that the goats went very fast,—faster than her mamma could walk, so that she had to stop sometimes to let her come up.

She had tried to make room for her inside the chaise, but mamma would not get in, so they went jogging on till, still in her dream, Rosy got very sleepy and tired, and wished that she were at home again.

This dream did not take long after all, though it sounds so long; and before it was done, the train had stopped, and mamma had got out and sent nurse to look after the boxes. Papa took Rosy's hand, and then they all walked down to the steamboat.

Mamma went to lie down in the ladies' cabin, and nurse went into the cabin where the nurses were, and Rosy was laid on a cushion beside her, where she soon fell asleep again, and slept nicely till the boat stopped.

Then papa came in to fetch her, and carried her on deck, and she saw the great wide sea with its rolling waves running after one another and tossing all the little boats about. She saw lots of boxes on board too, and lots of Englishmen putting them on to the shore, and the Frenchmen taking them and saying a great many words that Rosy could not understand, though she did know a little French, because her papa had taught her.

And very soon they were in a great room, full of little tables, and having their dinner with the other people who had been in the boat. And after dinner they got into a train once more. It was getting dark

' Papa had his little girl to carry, and he did not want her to wake.

then, and Rosy's bed-time. So she soon went fast asleep again. And when they got to the end of their journey, nurse took care of the boxes, for papa had his little girl to carry, and he did not want her to wake. And she never woke till she found herself in a strange bed next morning, and heard nurse telling her it was breakfast time.

CHAPTER IV.

IN FRANCE.

ROSY was so surprised ! She could not make it out at all, and she said :

'But I was in a boat yesterday, and then I was in a train ; how did I get here ?'

It took a long time to explain. But Rosy had slept in a very pretty little bed, which had curtains round it all covered with roses, and she had to ask a great many questions about that. It was a dear little bed, and Rosy wanted to know if she were to sleep in it always now. 'Oh no,' nurse said, ' we are not in our new home yet : there are more trains to come before we get there.'

‘ But I was in a boat yesterday, and then I was in a train.   How did I get here ? ’

So Rosy made haste to dress, and go down to her mamma, that she might find out all sorts of things. Papa told her that they were in Paris now, and that soon she should go out and see the fine streets and shops. The house belonged to an old friend of papa's. It was a funny old house, with trees round it, and quite away from the busy streets.

Her legs were too short to carry her a very long way; but she liked very much going into a toy-shop to buy a beautiful soft lamb, which her papa gave her to play with in the next train. And she was not very sorry when mamma took her into another shop to buy a pretty box of sweet things which the French call 'bon-bons.' There were some white, and some buff, and some pink ones; but Rosy was only allowed to taste one, because they were intended to amuse her when they went on again.

So when the little girl thought of all these nice things, she was not so sorry as before that the journey was not done yet, and did not feel so tired at the idea of ' trains again.'

But mamma was very tired and very poorly too, and papa had a great many friends to visit whom he had not seen for a long time. And they had not seen his little girl either; so they all stayed in Paris for a few days; and that was very nice.

One day Rosy was taken into a large house where there were a great many pictures. It was called a palace. Another day she walked in a very fine garden, and a third day she went to play with some little French girls and see their dolls.

That was a very funny visit, for they could only say a very little English, and Rosy could only speak a very little French; so they looked at each other and laughed, and pointed to things, and kissed one another, but did not talk much.

Then came the train journey again. It was not new now; and Rosy did get very tired. But her papa held her on his knee again, and let her look out of window; and then she played with her lamb and ate her sugar-plums, and tried to be a good girl.

They stopped again to see some other friends at a large, large town called Lyons, where lots of silks are made for ladies' dresses. Rosy's mamma took her to see how they were made, and a kind gentleman gave her a little piece of bright blue silk to make her doll a new frock.

D

Then came the last long ride, and Rosy was so tired this time that she could not help crying for a part of the way.

At last the train came close to the sea, and papa told her that now they would soon be there. She watched the boats on the sea, and thought how she would like to be in one of them. And she watched the great high hills as they seemed to run by them; and in the fields there were some very funny-looking sheep, so tall and with such long legs that they did not look like the sheep that Rosy used to see.

At last there came a very loud long whistle, and papa cried out:

'Here we are! Here we are in Cannes at last!'

Then there came a great bustle, and very soon papa, mamma and Rosy, were all sitting at lunch together in a pretty room which had a garden in front of it full of orange-trees.

Oh, what fun it was to see the oranges growing! Rosy was so fond of oranges; but unfortunately these were not ripe yet, they were still only green, and not yellow; so she must wait and watch them very patiently until they got ripe.

Now there was a little grass growing under the trees—not a regular grass-plot— it is too dry at Cannes for grass-plots such as we have in England; but still a little, growing tall and thin, and mixed with pretty wild flowers of many sorts, and much larger and brighter than she had ever seen growing wild before.

So after lunch was over Rosy slipped down off her chair, got on her mamma's lap, and whispered something. I dare say you will know what it was when I tell you that her mamma said 'yes,' and put on her little girl's hat again. At any rate it was not long before a little round maiden was to be seen stooping down under one of the largest trees and picking something as fast as her fat hands would move.

They seemed in a short time to have picked more than they could anyhow hold at once, for just when a splendid nosegay was coming together, down fell a lot of the very prettiest flowers from the side at which the blue eyes were not looking. And this happened two or three times until at last that fat little woman got quite impatient, and sitting down on the ground let all the red and pink and blue and yellow flowers tumble in a heap into her lap.

And as she let them fall she gave them a little slap and said:

'You naughty things! you are very tiresome. Rosy won't try any more, she won't.'

Then she covered them over with her frock, lest the wind should blow them all away, and held up her little head to see if any of the green oranges were getting just a little wee bit yellow.

She looked so longingly and so eagerly that there came a step closer and closer to her, and some one even sat down by her side, and put an arm all round her, before she guessed that any one was near. But it was a kind arm and a voice that she knew very well; for it was her own nursey who said:

'So Rosy has quite forgotten all about

'Try, try, try again,
You can do it if you try.'

'No, I can't nurse,' cried Rosy, 'I can't, I can't: they're naughty flowers and won't be tied together. I wanted to make a nose-gay for mamma; but they won't go up into a nosegay, they won't.'

'Then see if you can't make two instead of one, a nosegay for mamma and another for papa. Then there won't be so many together, and perhaps they won't quarrel so much.'

Rosy gave a merry laugh at the idea of flowers quarrelling, and set to work very busily to sort the flowers as nurse advised her.

First she picked out all the red ones and put them by themselves, then all the pink, and then the blue and yellow, and when she had got four heaps, she took half of each of them, and found that now she had a bunch which she could quite well hold in her fat hands,—yes, even in one hand—so she held it quite tight so that not one flower should tumble out while she wound the string which she had brought on purpose all the way from London, round and round and round them, and then asked nurse to tie the two ends.

But nurse said, ' No; she must try and do it all herself,' and told her to lay it carefully down, and have both hands free to tie the bow.

Rosy knew how to tie a bow; because she had learnt a good while ago. She did not like learning that, for at first the tape on which she learnt would keep coming undone; but nurse said then too, ' Try, try,

try,' and so Rosy was brave and did try. So now she could tie her nosegays up quite well when she had both hands free. And when she had made them both up, don't you think she was much more pleased to be able to say, ' I did them all myself,' than she would have been if she had gone in and said, ' Mamma, I began to make you a nosegay, but it won't do up at all?'

CHAPTER V.

VISIT TO THE DAIRY.

HEN Rosy opened her eyes the next morning the sun was shining so brightly that she was obliged to shut them again. But a great many thoughts came into her little head, and she was in a great hurry to get up.

Nurse said it was not time yet, and that she was very sleepy; but when the little girl had climbed into her bed, and given her a great many soft kisses, and told her how much she wanted to take a walk before breakfast, the kind nursey first rubbed her eyes, then opened them, and then got out of bed.

While she was dressing, Rosy began to put on her own shoes and stockings and some of her clothes; for she had already learnt to do a great deal for herself.

She peeped out of window to look for the birds, but for some time she could not see any.

Rosy thought this very strange, for she remembered how she used to hear the dear little birdies sing when she had been in the country in England; but nurse could not explain the puzzle; so Rosy settled that it was to be a question for her papa. Of course he would know; he always knew everything.

When they were quite ready nurse said: 'Now, my darling, if you like we will go and get your milk for breakfast; for I know where it is to be had, and nice, new, good milk I hope it may be, to make my little Trotty very fat.'

'Is not Rosy fat now?' asked the little girl in surprise, and feeling first her plump cheeks and then her round arms with her stumpy little fingers.

'Oh, pretty well,' said nurse laughing, 'but you may be fatter yet, and I like fat little girls.'

They had not to walk far before they came to the place where the milk was sold. It was called a farm; and nurse took Rosy in, and said she should see the dairy if the good woman would let her.

Rosy did not know what a dairy meant; but she supposed that it was something curious, and tripped merrily along, wondering what she should see, till they came to a room which had a floor made of red tiles, on which stood at least ten or twelve large open bowls full of new milk.

Now Rosy happened to be very fond of milk; and as she was just then quite ready for her breakfast, she was very pleased to have her mug filled,—the mug which she had brought on purpose, as nurse told her,—and then take a good drink.

'Ah, nurse, how good it is!' she cried, 'but, what is all this sticking to my lips? It is not white like our milk. See, there is something on the top of it;' and she held out her mug to show her.

'Ah, that's cream, good cream. We did not get milk like this in Paris,' said nurse; 'and I'm sure we don't in London. There's no water here; is there, madame?'

'She was very pleased to have her mug filled—the mug which she
had brought on purpose.'

But madame did not understand English; so nurse was obliged, by looking very pleased, to make her see that she thought her milk very good.

'But it's very bad of the other people to put water in my milk,' said Rosy frowning. 'I shall ask my papa to scold them when we go home; and I shall take a great mugful of this nice milk to show my grandmamma.'

'Well now say good-bye prettily in French as your papa teaches you,' said nurse, 'and then we'll go home, and I dare say we shall find some more milk there.'

'Adieu, madame,' said the little girl, and off she trotted again, as ready to go as she had been to come.

They say 'madame' to every one in

France, you know, and not to rich ladies only.

Now there are beautiful hills all round the back of Cannes, and a little way up one of these was the house where Rosy was going to live. She did so like running up and down hills; and there were two or three little ones between the farm and the house, which was called a villa.

When she got on to the top of one, she cried out:

'Ah, there's the sea, I do declare; and there's a boat on it with a white sail !   Shall we go in a boat some day ?'

'I don't know,' said nurse, 'you must ask your mamma; but you don't want to be sick, do you ?'

'I won't be sick,' cried the little girl. 'Rosy is never sick in a beau'ful boat like that. I'll ask my mamma,' and she bustled on.

' Stay, stay,' cried nurse, ' you're going too far, my pet, this is the way; look who stands up there ?'

Rosy looked up, and there was the villa with its green blinds high up over her head; and some one stood outside the door calling her by name.

Oh, what a number of steps there were for those little legs to climb, before she reached her papa !

They went up by the side of a garden, which was itself like a lot of wide steps, and on each step there was a row of vines, not trained against a wall as we train our vines in England, but growing on the ground like bean plants.

Rosy saw lots of such nice grapes that

her little mouth quite watered, and she would have liked to have stopped to pick some; but then she knew that would be stealing, because they were not hers. And I hope that Rosy would not have stolen even if nurse had not been following her, or her papa watching her.

She got the grapes, too, without picking them; for when she had climbed up to the very top, there was papa waiting for her with a beautiful bunch in his hand. And he said :

' Come in, Rosy, mamma wants her breakfast very badly. See, mamma, what a pair of roses your little girl has been getting already.'

Rosy knew very well what that meant, for she rubbed her cheeks with her little fat hands, and then tumbled her merry little head about her mamma's lap to 'roll the roses off,' as she said.

But that little head was too full of thoughts to stay there long.

There was so much to tell and to talk about, and that dairy took a long time to describe. Then when papa asked if she had seen the dear cows that gave the milk, she thought that that would be a capital little jaunt for to-morrow, and clapped her hands with glee.

'So you are going to find some new pets, Rosy,' he said, 'to do instead of Mr. Tommy and the kittens.'

'Ah, papa, but there are no dickies here, —I mean hardly any,' she answered. 'We looked so for the birdies all, all the time; but only two came, and went away again directly.'

E

'We must go out and see the reason of that,' said papa, smiling,—'you and I, Rosy, directly after breakfast. We must go and tell the dear birds that Rosy has come.'

CHAPTER VI.

A WALK AND A DRIVE.

ROSY made such haste to finish her bread and milk, that she was ready to go out before any one else had done breakfast. But her papa was not long before he was ready too, and she was soon tripping along by his side.

They went only a little way up the road, and then they came to a field, on one side of which were some high bushes. Rosy knew where to look for birds, and peeped very anxiously amidst the boughs till she saw something hopping. Then she pulled her papa's hand, and let him know that she wanted him to stoop down and look too.

He looked and then whispered :

'Yes, Rosy. There is a pretty little robin; let us go round the other side and see if we can make him come out with these crumbs which I have brought with me.'

So they went softly to the gate, and were just going in, when papa said,—

'Stop, Rosy; look what that man has got in his hand.'

Then she looked and saw a man with a very long gun and two dogs.

'What is he going to do, papa?' asked the little girl, drawing back; 'will he shoot us if we go in?'

'Oh, no, Rosy, don't be afraid.   It is

the robin that he wants to shoot and not us. So now you see how it is that the dicky-birds don't sing much at Cannes. It is because they shoot so many of them.'

Poor little Rosy! She loved so much to watch the little birds and hear them sing! And when she thought of this dear robin being shot quite dead, and that perhaps there was a nest somewhere with little ones who would have no mamma, she began to cry and to call the man 'a cruel fellow.' She was not much comforted by being told that such little birds were eaten there; so that if the man could shoot one, he would get some money for it which might buy bread for *his* little ones. But she was rather glad to hear that the little robins must be able by that time of year to take care of themselves, and had left the nest some time, — and much more pleased when, soon after, she saw the dear robin fly right away, so that the man with the gun was not likely to shoot that one at any rate.

Then papa said, 'I shouldn't wonder if mamma would like to go out this morning. Shall we go back and see?'

Rosy thought that would be very nice; and then her papa lifted up his little girl, and showed her all the beautiful hills that were behind them. There were some that had peaked tops, and some rather roundish; and just in one place she could see some hills a very long way off, that seemed to climb right up into the sky and were all white on the top. He told her that those hills were called mountains because they were so very high,—a great deal too high

'She was very much pleased when soon after she saw the robin fly right away.'

for Rosy to walk up, and that the white stuff which she saw was snow.

'We don't have snow when it is warm in England, Rosy, do we?' said papa, 'nor yet here, but up there, you see, it is so cold that the snow never melts. Those are called "the snow Alps."'

Rosy had nearly forgotten the poor birds now, because there were so many other things to think about. She saw some poppies a little way off, and then some blue flowers; and they were so pretty that she was quite obliged to stop a good many times to pick some for dear mamma. The wind was very high too, and it blew little Rosy's hat right off, so that papa and she had both to run after it.

Mamma was ready for a walk when they got in, but she stayed to put Rosy's flowers

in water; and they looked very gay and
pretty.   Nurse and every one admired them;
and Rosy said that she was not a bit tired,
and was quite sure that she could go for
another long, long walk.

But papa said that though Rosy might
be a little horse her mamma was not, and
that it was a long way to the town and to
the shops where she wanted to go; so he
would go and get a carriage for them.

Now, though Rosy certainly was very
tired of trains she found a basket pony carriage a very different thing, and enjoyed her
ride so much that she was obliged to change
pretty often from her mamma's lap to her
papa's and back again, just because she was
too happy to sit still.

The ponies went along merrily, too, as
if they were nearly as happy.   They had

bells on their necks which jingled delight-
fully, and every now and then they met
a carriage, or even a cart, the horses of
which had bells too.   So they had plenty of
music.

They went up one hill and down another,
and the ponies ran so fast, and turned round
the corners of the roads so quickly, that
sometimes mamma was afraid that the carriage would be upset, and that they would
all be 'tipped out in a heap.'   Rosy thought
it would be good fun if they were.   She often
rolled about herself like a little ball without
hurting herself; and she thought that papa
and mamma would only get a little dusty,
and that it would be a nice little job for
her to brush the dust off when she got
home.

Just then a number of boys and girls

came along the road to meet them, and
Rosy saw that all the little ones wore caps,
not hats or bonnets.   There was one baby
with large black eyes, whom she would have
liked to kiss and hug.   It was so fat and
pretty.   But it was dressed in a way that
she had never seen any baby dressed before,
for its feet and legs were put into a sort of
large bag, so that it could not kick like other
children ; and Rosy wondered how it could
laugh so merrily.

When the carriage came near this little
party the man did not hold the reins of his
horses tight as an English coachman would
have done.   He only screamed out to the
children, ' Gare, gare,' which Rosy's papa
told her meant ' Get out of the way.'

And when they were all passed there
came next a great waggon, piled up with

the trunks of trees. The horses which drew this had no bells; but they had a funny sort of post sticking up high between their ears, with lots of things hanging on to it. They had also three pink tassels hanging on their faces, one in front, and one on each side. These tassels shook as they went along, and looked so pretty that Rosy thought to herself that if ever she had a toy horse again she would ask nurse to make some little tassels for it just like them. Her papa had told her, too, that they were to keep off the flies which teased the poor horses very often dreadfully. And of course Rosy would not like her horse to be teased.

But the carriage went on while she was thinking this; and soon they saw four old women coming along the road with large baskets, full of some green stuff, on their

heads.   The little girl did not say anything
as they went by, but she looked very particularly to see how they were dressed.

Now I must tell you why she did
this.

In the first place, then, she had never
seen any old women a bit like them before.

They walked all in a row with their
baskets on their heads, and their hands stuck
into their sides ; and they talked very fast as
they came along.   On their heads they wore
very, very large hats, with small crowns.
Rosy had never seen such hats before, and
she heard her mamma say that she had never
seen them either.   Under these great hats
they had nice white caps, with coloured
handkerchiefs over them, which hung down
behind.   They had besides other coloured

handkerchiefs over their shoulders, and two of them had red gowns.

Now Rosy had had a present given her in Paris. It was a piece of French money worth ten English pennies; and with this money she had bought ten Dutch dolls, which nursey was going to dress for her. At first she meant them to make an English school; but now that she had seen so many funny people she thought she would like her dolls to be dressed like the people in Cannes, because then they would just show her dear grandmamma how very nice they looked, and how very different to English people.

She was very quiet for a little while because she was making this grand plan; but they soon turned out of the narrow street, and all at once she saw the sea again.

They had come now to what was called
the 'port,' and there were all the great ships
which had come home lately, and were waiting to go out again ; one, two, three, four,
five, six, all in a row, quite quiet, and 'taking
their naps,' as Rosy's papa said, 'after all
their hard work.'

He lifted Rosy out first and said that
they would go and look at them, while
mamma went into the shops.

Rosy was not quite sure whether she was
pleased at that, because sometimes her mamma bought her very nice things, such as toys,
or sugar-plums, or cakes, when she took her
out shopping.   But they soon found plenty
to look at, and some funny men with blue
coats and cocked hats amused the little girl
very much.   Her papa wondered why she
looked at them so often, but then he did

not know **Rosy's** grand scheme, and how she was thinking of asking nurse to dress one doll just like them. She kept this little plan quite a secret till she got back to her nurse.

It was half the fun to have a secret.

CHAPTER VII.

ROSY'S VISIT TO THE COWS.

THE dear, good nursey did not forget about the cows next morning, for when Rosy opened her little blue peepers there she was half dressed.

Rosy jumped up in a minute, crying out,——

'The cows! the cows! Shall we go and see them?'

'If you will make great haste,' said the nurse, 'but it is getting late.'

Rosy never got dressed more quickly. She did not much like even to wait for her morning splash; and while her curls were being combed, she kept saying, ' Won't it do, nurse?' and then rather hindering by holding up her little face for a kiss.

As soon as she was quite ready she bustled off and got down-stairs first. Whom should she see there but papa himself, with his hat on?

He said that he would take her to see the cows, and even carry her a little way if she got tired.

How very kind that was! But would such a great girl as Rosy get tired?

Oh dear, no; at least, so she said, for Rosy did not like to be thought a baby now, though, somehow or other, it did sometimes happen that after a long walk her feet would ache a little bit, and then papa's shoulder made a very comfortable seat.

F

She was half afraid now that nursey might be sorry not to see the cows, and ran back to whisper that if she liked she might dress one of the dollies instead. That was meant for a treat, you know; and nursey laughed, and said,—

'Perhaps, we shall see;' and gave her another kiss.

Then Rosy showed her papa where the farm was; and when they came near, they saw the farmer's wife standing at the door, as if she expected her little visitor.

Rosy did not forget to say,—

'Bon jour, madame,' which means 'good morning' in English, you know.

Papa asked in French if they could see the cows, and the good woman was kind enough to take them round to the water where they were drinking.

There was a black one, and a black and white one, and a red one, and another with red spots. We cannot find room for them all in the picture; but you will see the one which was drinking.

Rosy admired them very much, and wanted to go as near as she could that she might see them well; for although they were so very big and had such long legs, she was not a bit afraid of them. She never was afraid of anything when her papa was by because he was so very strong,—stronger than all the world she thought.

'Who made the cows, Rosy?' asked her papa, when she had looked at them a little while.

'God,' said Rosy, softly; 'God made everything, didn't He, papa? Why did He make the cows?' she asked, after thinking a minute.

'To give us good milk, such as you had yesterday, Rosy, and to make you and other little girls and boys fat and strong. Was not that very good of God?'

'Yes, papa,' said Rosy, again.

'Then will you remember that, my little one, when you say by-and-by, "I thank God for my nice bread and milk?"'

Rosy said she would, and then she asked,—

'And do the pretty cows give us coffee, too, papa?'

'No, no, my silly little Rosy; don't you recollect that we buy that at the grocer's shop? We must go some day and ask them to let you see it ground up to powder. The coffee comes from a long, long way off. It

' And do the pretty cows give us coffee too, papa?'

grows on a tree in a very hot country and looks like little berries till they put it into a mill and turn a handle. Then the berries are ground up to powder, and we put some boiling water over the powder, and when it gets cool we drink it. Haven't you seen mamma pour it out into the cup and put some sugar and milk in for herself and papa?'

Rosy remembered now; but she had not taken much notice before because she did not like coffee at all. She liked her nice milk much better; and so when she went away with her papa she called out,—

'Good-by, dear cowies; and thank you very much for my nice milk.'

Rosy wanted to walk round the other side where there was a very gentle, kind-looking cow, that was not in the water, because she thought that she would like to stroke her; but her papa told her to look at those two great horns. And he said that cows did not like little girls to take liberties with them unless they knew them, and that this cow did not know her, and might think her very saucy, and poke out her horns to teach her to keep a proper distance. If she did, he said he thought Rosy would not like that poke, for it might hurt her, so he advised her to keep quite out of the good cow's way.

Then she stood at a little distance to watch her drinking, and Rosy's papa said,—

'See how she enjoys it! Cows like to come here sometimes, like little girls; but French cows don't get out of their houses so often as English ones.'

'Don't they, papa?' said Rosy. 'Then I should think they must often wish to go to England.'

Papa laughed, and said,——

'Perhaps they would wish it if they knew how their English cousins enjoy themselves; but I think they look pretty happy; don't you, Rosy?'

Rosy said,——

'Yes, papa; but how funnily the cow drinks! She puts her head into the water.'

'And you think that if she were a polite cow she would not think of doing such a vulgar thing, but would wait till they gave her a glass; eh, Rosy?'

'She hasn't got any hands, papa,' cried Rosy, 'so she couldn't, I 'pose.'

'No,' said papa; 'so I think that we

must excuse and forgive the poor thing,
until Rosy can teach her a better plan.'

And Rosy trotted home by his side,
thinking how much she should like to try
drinking after the cow's fashion.

CHAPTER VIII.

ROSY'S VISIT TO THE HENS.

ROSY was very hungry when she got home to breakfast, for the fresh morning air had given her an appetite.

Her mamma took off her hat and her little jacket and said,—

'So, Rosy, you have brought me two more roses.'

'But my roses don't smell, mamma,' said Rosy, laughing and patting her own fat cheeks, as she always did when mamma said that. Then she made haste to scramble up on to her little chair, and pull her nice basin

of bread and milk close to her.   She looked
at her papa after she had said her little grace
and said,—

'I didn't forget, papa.'

Then she began to eat away as if she
liked it very much, and when she had eaten
a little her mamma said,—

'Look here, Rosy.'

And Rosy turned round and saw a
whole spoonful of egg waiting for her
to eat it.   Mamma was holding it for
her; and it looked so yellow and so delicious !

Rosy opened her mouth, but she did
not take it all in at once.   It was too good
for that, and she thought it better to make
it last a little.

But some of the yellow would stick on
Rosy's lips; so mamma wiped it off, and

then Rosy put her arms round her neck and kissed her, and said,—

'So nice, dear mamma.'

Then mamma said,—

'At the end of the garden, Rosy, there lives the good hen that gave us this nice egg, and a great many other hens and very fine cocks too,—the cocks that you heard crowing this morning. Shall we go and see them after breakfast?'

'Oh, yes, yes, yes!' cried Rosy, clapping her hands, 'that will be fun. I've almost done mine;' and the little girl made great haste to finish her bread and milk; but mamma said,—

'Ah, but not quite directly. I've not done my breakfast. If you have done yours, you had better go and see what nurse is doing, and ask her to get ready to come and hear papa read about Daniel in the lions' den.'

Rosy did not mind waiting for that, for she was never tired of hearing that story. I dare say that some of her young friends know it too.

Her mamma got ready soon after, and they both went round to a part of the garden which Rosy had not seen before.

There they saw that one piece was railed off from all the rest, and that a hen-house was inside it.

Rosy's mamma opened a gate in the railing and took her little girl into the enclosure amongst all the cocks and hens.

The cocks did not seem much to like this, and they both made a great crowing, and then marched off into the farthest corner with a lot of hens after them.

Rosy said,—

'Oh, mamma, show them the nice seed, and then they won't go away.'

But her mamma answered,—

'Not yet, Rosy; let us go first and look at these good ladies that are walking about inside their house. We can have a good look at them before they get away. See, they can't get out 'if we stand at the door.'

'Ah, look at these beauties all over speckly feathers,' cried Rosy as she ran forward to catch one.

She put out her little arms to seize her; but the hen seemed to think this a great liberty from so small a child, and instead of running away she turned and opened her beak in a very angry manner.

'Take care, Rosy,' said her mamma, as

the little girl drew back half frightened. 'This hen seems rather a fierce lady. I will give her some seed to persuade her to be quiet. Perhaps she has got something there that she does not choose us to see. I wonder what it can be.'

Rosy took one more peep and then called out, —

'Oh, mamma, mamma, some little chickens, I do declare. If you stoop down you can see them running about behind her, — such dear, pretty, soft, little creatures! Do get me one to play with.'

'Little chickens!' said mamma; 'why they must have come out of their shells very late in the year if they are little ones still, and I am afraid their mother won't let me touch them.'

'Do chickens come out of shells?' said

Rosy, making very large eyes, and looking quite puzzled.

' Yes, Rosy, out of just such shells as our eggs had this morning; and if in the summer we had given this good hen five or six of her own eggs in this little house of hers, she would have sat upon them and spread her wings over them to keep them warm; and there she would have stayed so patiently all day long, and day after day until the dear little chickens were ready to come out.'

' And wouldn't the hen get tired?' said Rosy. ' I shouldn't like to stay still so long.'

' No, I don't think you would,' said her mamma, chucking her little girl under the chin; ' but then you see you are like the little chickens, and not like the mamma hen,

I think you will find that she has not got tired even yet, for if you peep down again you will see that she is keeping two of the little chickens warm under her even now. Little chickens are like little babies, and they very soon get cold, so they like keeping very close to their mammas.'

'Are the little chickens naughty sometimes?' asked Rosy.

'Well I don't know, Rosy; but I know that I have often thought it very pretty to see how they will all run to their mother when the great hen clucks for them.'

'Oh, mamma, I should *so* like to hear her cluck,' cried Rosy, clapping her hands.

'Well, Rosy, you go a little way off, and keep quite quiet; and then I will see if I can tempt the good lady out of her nest with some of this nice seed.'

'If you stoop down you will see that she is keeping two of the little chickens warm under her.'

So Rosy ran away, and her mamma stepped back a few paces and threw down some of the seed. The hen saw it directly and looked for an instant as if she would like some very much; and she did not wait long, but soon stepped out of her house, and began picking up the seed.

Just at that moment a cat came creeping along the outside of the paling, and watching to see if she could pounce on one of the little chickens. The hen saw the cat and began to stretch out her neck very fiercely, as if she meant to fly at its eyes, and then began to cluck for her little ones, which all came running to her as fast as their legs would carry them.

Rosy's little eyes sparkled with pleasure, and she went up and put her hand into her mamma's and said softly,—

G

' Wasn't it nice ?'

' Yes, Rosy,' said her mamma, ' and I hope that my little chicken will always run to my side as quickly as these did to their mother. You see she knew that they were in danger when they didn't themselves; and so do I sometimes when my Rosy thinks she is quite safe.'

CHAPTER IX.

THE LITTLE DUCKS.

SHALL we go out this way and take a little walk, or go back again to the house and have our reading-lesson, Rosy?' asked her mamma, when they had seen enough of the poultry-yard.

'Ah, for a walk, please, dear mamma,' said the little girl, who did not feel much inclined for lessons at that moment.

'Very well, Rosy,' answered mamma; 'and I suppose my little girl will prefer to have holidays all the while she stays at Cannes, and would not mind going back to tell grandmamma that she cannot read one bit better than when she left England.'

'Oh, yes, mamma; but I should mind a great deal,' said Rosy, quickly, ''cause—'

'Because of what, Rosy?' asked her mamma.'

''Cause Rosy *promised* to learn much, much,' said the child, giving two or three little jumps; 'but please, a walk now, dear mamma.'

So mamma and Rosy went out at the back gate, and came into a field which had a little stream running at the end of it. There was a hen, too, near the edge of this stream making such a loud cackling and screaming that Rosy said she thought she must be crying.

She ran a little way on and came back in a great hurry to say that some of the good little chickens had tumbled in, and to beg her mamma to 'come quick and get them out.'

Mamma went on as fast as she could walk, but she said,—

'I think you are mistaken, darling; I don't think that what you see are chickens.'

'Oh, yes, mamma, they are, they are indeed; look at the poor old hen.'

Rosy got to the edge of the stream first. She did not go very near because her mamma called to her to stop, and she remembered how the little chickens had done as their mother told them at the very first cluck. Perhaps if Rosy had forgotten this, and had gone a little further, she might have tumbled in, and that would have been a sad thing indeed.

But she stopped just behind the poor

hen, who was in a terrible fright, and before her mamma could come up Rosy had
begun to cry.

'Oh, mamma, what can we do? what
shall we do?' sobbed the little one.
'They'll all die, they'll all be drowned; they
will, they will!'

'No, Rosy, they won't hurt, you need
not fret about them,' said her mamma, sitting down on a bank beside her. 'These
are not chickens at all, but young ducks.
If we wait a minute we shall see that they
will swim nicely, and then the poor hen
won't be frightened at all.'

Rosy's mamma was quite right, for the
young ducks soon began to swim about
bravely and as if they had been used to the
water all their lives; and when the old hen
saw that, though she looked very much sur-

' No, Rosy, they won't hurt ; you need not fret about them.'

prised at first, yet she soon left off calling them, and became tolerably quiet.

Then Rosy's mamma put her arm round her little girl, and said,—

'Shall I tell you, Rosy, how this came about?'

'Yes, do, please, mamma; tell Rosy a story.'

'Well then, Rosy, I suppose this good hen had some eggs of her own, for see here are some little chickens that never tried to go into the water. And then there must have been a duck who had some eggs, too. Perhaps the hen and the duck were friends; and I fear the poor duck must have got ill and died. But the farmer's wife wanted some young ducks as well as some young chickens, so she did not let the eggs be eaten up, —as we ate ours this morning,—but put them all into a nest and set the hen to sit on them. I don't know what the hen thought about the little ducks, I'm sure; perhaps she may have thought them a rough sort of chicken, and hoped that they would get better, like other chickens, as they grew older, but I suppose she loved them very much indeed and took great care of them. They can never have seen water, we may be sure, before to-day: and now somebody must have left the gate open for a little while, and so the old hen got out with all her little brood.   Perhaps she was very pleased to get so much liberty; but I think she must soon have wished that she had stayed at home; for no doubt as soon as the duck-lings saw the water they knew that it was just the thing for them; so in they tumbled in spite of all the old hen's clucks, and

now see how they are enjoying themselves.'

'But it was very naughty of them,' cried
Rosy. 'They are bad little ducks, and I
don't love them at all.'

Her mamma smiled, and said,—

'The old hen wasn't really their mother,
you see, she was more like your good nursey.
It would be very wrong to do what nursey
told you not to do, wouldn't it, Rosy?
and I hope you will never give her such a
fright.'

Rosy was sure she never could be so unkind; and they both began to scramble up
a hill till they came to some trees that looked
something like willow-trees, only that there
were lots of green fruit upon them, such as
Rosy had never seen before.

The fruit was about the size of a small

nut; and there were men underneath beating the trees to make it fall down.

'See, Rosy,' said her mamma, 'these are olive-trees. Do you remember ever hearing of such trees before?'

'Oh, yes, in the Bible, mamma,' cried Rosy. 'You did read to me one Sunday about the Mount of Olives, and Jesus going out there when he was going up to heaven. And I saw a picture, too, of the garden where the olives grew. That was in my new Bible stories, you know. Will you read me the story about that picture some day, mamma?'

'Yes, Rosy, this evening at bed-time, if you like. But that garden was not in this country, you know. It was near Jerusalem, where the temple was, and where Jesus used to go to teach the people.'

'I didn't think we should see olives here, mamma. Are they good to eat?'

'Oh, yes, some people like them very much; but I don't think my little girl would like them, because they are so bitter. The people grow them here for the sake of the oil which they get out of them.'

'I don't like oil,' said Rosy, making a great face.

'Oh, but this is not like castor oil. Some of the poor people like it very much. Shall we go and see what those people are doing who are sitting down under that wall?'

The people whom they saw were some men and women who had been working in the fields, and now they were having their dinners, as Rosy's mamma guessed.

So she went up to them and asked them if they would like to have some pretty little books which she took out of her pocket. They looked as if they would, but spoke in such a funny way that Rosy's mamma could hardly understand anything they said, though she knew French quite well. She made out at last that there was a girl at home who could read quite well, so some of the little books were sent for her to read to the others.

'Will she like them?' asked Rosy, after they had got out of hearing.

'Yes; I think so, Rosy,' said her mamma, 'for I dare say she does not often get new books. Some little girls and boys, you see, are never taught to read at all, and no one reads to them either the stories that you like to hear me read, about Moses and David, or even about Jesus Christ, and how He came down from heaven to save sinners.'

'Did they like me to see them having their dinner?' said Rosy.

'I don't think they minded at all. French people are very fond of having a little chat. Did you see what they were having for dinner?'

'I saw some bread, great large pieces,' said Rosy, 'and something in a dish. What was that, mamma; was it gravy?'

'No, not gravy; that was oil, Rosy. Didn't you see how they dipped their bread into it, and how they seemed to like it?'

'I shouldn't,' said Rosy, giving a great shudder. 'How horrid! They had got a bottle and a mug, too,—only one mug for all of them. What was in the bottle?'

'Wine,' answered her mamma.

Rosy opened her eyes again very wide, and said,—

'Wine, mamma! but papa said one day that poor people couldn't have wine 'cause it costs such lots of money.'

'That was in England. This wine does not cost much, Rosy, and it does not make people tipsy. I wonder if nursey will like it instead of her beer.'

'And they had no meat and no potatoes,' said Rosy, with a sigh. 'Shall we go home and tell papa about the poor people?'

'Yes, if you 're tired, dear.'

And so mamma and her little girl went home to talk of what they had seen.

CHAPTER X.

HISTORY OF THE FALLEN PEARS.

THE garden belonging to the house where Rosy stayed was a nice large one; and it had lots of beautiful flowers, and lots of bushes with flowers on them, growing in different parts of it, and some trees, too, beside the orange-trees which I told you about before.

There were almond-trees and fig-trees, a few olive-trees, and two pear-trees.

Rosy liked pears very much, but these were a very late sort, and were not yet ripe.

A great wind blew for two nights and

days, and then came some rain; and after that Rosy went out again to play in the garden.

She went, first of all, to see whether the oranges were getting ripe, and then she went on to the pear-trees, and what do you think she saw? Oh, such a number of them lying on the ground.

Did Rosy want to eat them? Not at first. But she thought of some little pigs that Cecile the housemaid had told her about, and how much they liked to have the pears which fell off the trees, and then she ran in to ask if she might pick up some and carry them in her pinafore to their little house.

Her papa saw her coming, and went out to hear what she wanted. And he said,—

'Yes, Rosy, you may; but, mind, they are only ripe enough for pigs.'

So Rosy went back, and had great fun for a little while in picking them up, and thinking how the pigs would like them. She had a basket with her, for her papa had given her one to put them in; and soon it was nearly full of small green pears which did not look so very tempting as to make her wish to eat them. But just when she had got it nearly full, she spied a large pear which looked as if it must be quite ripe. She did not put that into her basket at once, but looked at it all round and round, squeezed it, and patted it, and at last smelt it.

That was a very dangerous thing to do, because, of course, it smelt very nice. And then Rosy thought to herself, 'It must be

H

ripe, I'm sure. It wouldn't have that rosy cheek if it weren't. I wish papa would come and say I might eat it. He would if he were here, I know.'

And when she had thought all these things, the little girl, all on a sudden, took a great bite, and said to herself that when it was all gone she would tell her papa just how it was, and that if he knew it was ripe, he wouldn't mind; she was quite sure of that.

But when she had taken two bites, Rosy began to think that it was rather hard, and something seemed to say, ' It isn't ripe, you know.'

She didn't listen though, but took some more bites until, all at once, just in the middle of the fruit, what should she spy but a great caterpillar, with a lot of brown stuff all round him ?

'When she had thought all these things, all on a sudden she took a great bite.'

Oh, she let it fall so quickly, and was so sorry then that ever she had tasted it. It made her feel quite sick to think that she might have gone on and bitten that caterpillar in half!

She was half inclined to cry, and stood for some time looking at the bitten pear which she had let fall. Then it came into her head that those great unripe pieces which she had swallowed would certainly make her ill; and then she thought that what she had done would all be found out, and every one would be angry with her.

When she began to bite the pear she had quite intended to tell, and to say that she knew she might because it was so ripe; but now she had found out that it was not ripe, and besides she began to remember how often before her mamma had said that she must not taste any fruit without leave.

Oh, Rosy, Rosy! how glad she would have been then if she had minded what her mamma said to her. She couldn't bear having this bad secret to keep——she had never had such a one before——and yet she was afraid to tell it.

At last she took up her basket-load which was almost too heavy for her to manage, and began to walk slowly towards the kitchen-door that she might ask Cecile to show her where the little pigs lived. But the pears would not stay in the basket; it was too full, and first one, and then another tumbled out. She picked them up and picked them up, and at last sat down on the ground and began to cry.

The little girl had thought herself quite

alone all this time; but she was not. Her papa was quite near to her, walking behind some bushes. He could see her, though she could not see him; and he wanted to see whether she would remember to be good when no one was by; so he kept out of her sight till he saw her sit down sobbing.

When Rosy saw him come from behind the bushes, she let go her basket which tumbled over and upset, and began to cry and sob more than ever.

She did not know that he had seen everything, and she wanted him to know, yet was afraid to tell. So, though he asked a great many times,—

'What is the matter, Rosy?' he got no answer except sobs.

Her papa had been sitting by his little

girl, and had put his arm round her while he asked her this question; but at last he said that if Rosy would not tell him he must go away and leave her by herself.

Rosy could not bear this, so she seized hold of his coat and whispered something which no one else could hear even if any one had been by.

Then papa looked very grave and said,—

'Ah, Rosy, I saw, though you did not know it.'

And Rosy said,—

'I so sorry. Rosy'll never do so again. Please kiss Rosy.'

And papa gave her a kiss, and took her up in his arms to carry her into the house; but he said,—

' The poor little pigs must go without their pears to-day, because Rosy has not been good enough to feed them.'

CHAPTER XI.

THE PIGS.

OF course mamma wondered when she saw Rosy come in crying, and nurse wondered too; and when they heard all about it, and said that they ' *thought* they could have trusted their little girl,' it made her more sorry than ever. It was very sad, too, to think of the little piggies losing their treat. Rosy thought that she would much rather have gone without her own tea; but she was afraid to say so.

To tell the truth, she had thought a great deal about this visit to the pig-sty ever since

Cecile had told her about the great sow with her fifteen little ones. And she thought about them all the afternoon, though she did not say anything, and she wondered whether she had told them of the treat they were to have, and whether they would be very much disappointed.

Mamma and nurse had quite forgiven her after she had said she was sorry, and then they did not talk any more about what she had done, until it came to her bed-time.

Rosy's mamma often came and sat by her bed for a little while after she had been tucked up. Sometimes she said hymns to her, and sometimes she talked a little about God who was her great Father up in heaven, who took care of her all night long, and who was always by her side.

She did not come in smiling as she often

did, on this evening, but she looked rather grave and sad; and she told her little girl that she had come to teach her just one little text out of the Bible.

'Thou, God, seest me;' that was the text.

It was only four words long; and Rosy had to say them over until she knew them quite well.

Her mamma did not tell her *why* she made her learn this; but Rosy knew very well; and when she had said it several times she put her arms round her neck and said again,—

'I so sorry.'

Can you guess what her kind mamma did then? I will tell you.

First she gave her little girl a kiss, and then she taught her to say to her great Father in heaven how very sorry she was for having forgotten that He saw her, and for doing such a bad thing, and ask Him to forgive her for the sake of her dear Saviour, who had died that she might have her sins forgiven.

Rosy did not feel so sad after that, and before she went to sleep she asked,—

'May I go and feed the pigs to-morrow?'

Her mamma said she might if it were fine, and soon afterwards Rosy fell asleep thinking what dear pretty creatures those piggies would be.

It was a splendid day; and as she had promised, Cecile came to take her to the pig-sty about ten o'clock. When she got to the gate of the yard round the sty, Rosy said,—

'Now let me go all by myself.'

So Cecile let go her hand, and Rosy went on, feeling as if she were a very great girl, because she had such a large present for the little animals.

She did not much like the place that she had to walk over; for the stones were very large and rough, and not at all clean. She wondered that some one did not sweep them or wash them very often;—for this little girl was rather particular about having things clean. She did not like dirty hands and dirty pinafores as some small people of her age seem to do.

When she got a little nearer she found another thing that she did not like one bit, and that was a very bad smell.

If it had not been that she saw the pigs just in front and was sure that they were in a great hurry for their pears, I think she

' She did not much like the place she had to walk over.'

would have run back again, she disliked it so much.

As it was she said to herself a great many times, ' Oh, what a horrid nasty smell ! ' and put her pinafore up to her nose.

When she got quite close she saw such a number of snouts sticking up, and then she heard Cecile call to her,—

' Don't go too close, missy. Don't put them into their mouths with your fingers, for fear they should bite you and make you dirty. Throw them in just like balls.'

Rosy was not sorry to do that, for now she wanted to get back as quickly as she could, away from that dirty place and out of that horrid smell.

Besides she was very much disappointed to find that the pigs were not at all the pretty creatures that she had fancied them.

She did not like their long snouts, but
thought them like very ugly noses. They
grunted too, and pushed one another about,
and rolled in the mud till they made themselves quite dirty. And then one had little
eyes, and another long flapping ears, and
another put his feet into the place where
his food was kept; and besides, Rosy could
not persuade them to divide their pears at
all fairly; so she called to Cecile to come
and help her; but Cecile could not manage
much better than she had done; for when
she threw a pear right across to one small
piggy who had come badly off, another
would come and take it from him; so
they were obliged to go and leave them
scrambling.

Rosy was not sorry to have some one to
lead her back over those slippery stones, and

she told Cecile that the only thing that she liked were those funny little curling tails, and that she thought it was a good thing that pigs didn't come into the houses like pusses and dogs.

But Cecile said that some people thought differently, for nurse told her that in Ireland she had seen a great pig who lived in a cottage amongst a lot of children as if he had been one of them, and that all the children petted him, and were very fond of him indeed.

' Oh,' said Rosy, putting her hand over her nose, ' I'm glad I didn't live with them. What are pigs for?' she added. ' I wish there were no pigs.'

You see that this little woman changed her mind rather quickly.

' What are they for?' returned Cecile.

'Why to make bacon and ham and pork of, to be sure. Don't you like ham?'

'Oh, yes, I do, much, much,' said Rosy, rubbing her hands together and looking up at Cecile as if her mouth watered at the thought. 'Will papa have ham for breakfast to-morrow?'

'That's more than I can say; but now you know what pigs are like, of course you won't eat any if he offers you a taste?'

'Oh, yes, I shall; I like ham; but how do they make the pigs clean enough? Do they wash them very, very often?'

'I've seen the hams hung up in a chimney to get a nice smoky taste,' returned Cecile, 'but I never saw them washed. They may be though, for aught I know.'

'In a chimney, Cecile! Oh, you're only teasing, I know. I'll ask my papa,' replied Rosy, in a positive little way that she sometimes used when she had an idea that people were imposing on her.

'And do you think that your papa knows how to cure hams, my little lady?' asked Cecile laughing.

'Of course he does,' said Rosy again, 'papa knows everything.'

CHAPTER XII.

THE WOODEN SHOES.

ROSY'S mamma sometimes went shopping and took her little girl with her. Little girls and boys too, you know, are apt to wear out their clothes in the country, and particularly their shoes. When they are at the sea-side, I dare say you know how often they want new ones. Well, Rosy was very fond of going on to the beach to play in the sand and to pick up shells. She found some very pretty ones, and her dear nurse made a very pretty little card-basket, which she lined with pink, and stuck all round with these shells. It was intended for her dear grandmamma; and if Rosy could find some more shells they were to be made into pretty things for presents for her cousins. So, you see, she wanted to find a great many; and when she was looking, sometimes her feet would get wet with the waves, which did not do the shoes any good.

I don't know that Rosy exactly minded the shoes being wet. In her heart, I rather fancy that she thought it very good fun when the waves caught her; but there was one thing which she did not like. It was being told that she ought not to wear out her shoes and boots so fast because they cost a great deal of money.

Now Rosy was a child that was rather fond of getting up little plans of her own; and I am going to tell you of one for saving her shoes which she thought such a very grand one that it kept her awake a whole half-hour one evening after she had been put to bed.

I told you -before that she sometimes went shopping with her mamma. Well, often when they had done with the shops, they used to go and sit on a bench near the market stalls, which are between the shops and the sea.

This was Rosy's favourite spot, because there was always so much to see. Such numbers of curious people came there, and such funny things were sold to eat.

There were lots of olives, and lots of grapes; and there were besides the berries of some jujube-trees, which grow in some parts of the town. Rosy loved jujubes with all her heart; but she never knew before what they were made of. However, she did not think the berries half as nice as the jujubes, which she had often eaten.

Well, one day while she was sitting by her mamma, watching the men and women selling, and the funny little children of her own age playing about in their funny baby caps, there came by a big girl riding on a donkey, between two very large panniers.

The girl had come out of the country with things to sell, and she had on a pair of shoes which took Rosy's fancy immensely. They were made of wood, and not a bit like what the other girls or women wore.

The girl got down off her donkey and talked a great deal to it, just as if it could understand, and were an old friend. Then she fastened it to a tree and came up to a stall near to where Rosy and her mamma were sitting, and as she walked along her shoes, which were made of wood, went 'plock, plock.'

The little girl thought it was a nice noise, and she got down and tried to do the same with her own little shoes, but they would only go 'pitter patter, pitter patter.'

Rosy's mamma began to talk to the girl and to ask her what she had to sell and where she lived; but the girl spoke a funny language, not like French at all, but like what the peasants spoke whom they had seen dining, and Rosy's mamma could not make her understand much that she said.

All the while she was talking Rosy was thinking of her shoes, and wondering whether she might have a pair just like them. And when the girl had gone away to buy something at a stall further on, Rosy only talked of her shoes. She did not *ask* for a pair like them then ; but when she went home she thought about it a great deal, and when she was lying on her little bed that night she made up her plan, that she would coax mamma to go again on the next day that the girl was to come, and then coax again to have a pair of shoes just like hers.

Rosy's mamma was rather amused at her little girl's fancy, but she said,—

' If they do not cost too much you may have them instead of the cart which I was going to buy you, if you like.'

Now Rosy had wanted this cart very much, but she wanted the shoes much more. She told her mamma they would be so strong, that she thought of the nice noise, and made up her mind at once.

So the girl was asked to bring a pair the size of Rosy's foot ; and Rosy went home full of joy to tell her nursey. She always told her everything, or very nearly everything, and nurse was always pleased when Rosy came home happy and good, but she said, —

'What a funny plaything to choose; if I had been a little girl I would have chosen the pretty cart to draw about the nursery.'

'Oh, but,' cried Rosy, ' the shoes will be so useful. They are so high, — so high as that, — nurse,' putting her hand a good way from the ground. 'I shall look like a big girl; and they make such a beautiful noise.'

And Rosy clapped her hands and ran all round the nursery because she was so glad and happy.

Well, the shoes came in good time, and Rosy went out into the garden to try them.

' At first, she felt afraid of falling, and was obliged to go slowly and carefully.'

She had seen the market girl run quite fast in them, and she meant to set off in the same way herself; but they were heavier than she had thought before she tried them on. At first she felt afraid of falling, and she was obliged to go slowly and carefully, so that no one would have taken her for the little merry skipping girl whom they had known before. Cecile came to look at her, as she tried to walk about in the heavy, clumsy shoes; and even the cat seemed as if it could not make it out.

But Rosy did not like to confess that mamma and nurse had been in the right when they said her own shoes were better; so she tried hard to manage them, and said she should get used to them in a little while.

They made her ankles ache, it was true; but she bore that for a good while without saying anything about it, and could not be persuaded to have them taken off until it was time to go down after her papa and mamma's dinner. She wanted to be able to wear them on the beach where they might get wet without being hurt; and when she had taken a thing into her little head it took a good deal to drive it out again.

So nurse said nothing, for though she was sorry to see her darling bearing so much pain she liked to see her *persevere*, that is, *try hard*, to do a thing.

But when Rosy had got them off, and her own nice little shoes on instead, she could not help saying that the thin ones were better for indoors.

You see it was not easy for her to keep any of her feelings in her own little heart.

CHAPTER XIII.

ADVENTURE WITH THE SHEEP.

THE house which Rosy's papa had taken was not quite in the town among the houses and shops, but a little way up one of the hills where there were nice fields all round.

Rosy never got tired of running about those fields, picking flowers, and watching the beautiful insects that flew about them. She was very fond of butterflies, and sometimes she used to want to catch them, until one day her mamma picked up a dead one, and showed her that the wings were all

covered with very tiny feathers, and that no
one could touch them without hurting them
very much.   She told her also that they
were very happy among the flowers, and
would be very unhappy if they were kept
shut up under a glass; and when Rosy had
remembered how little she would like to be
a poor little prisoner she thought she would
never try to catch them any more.

There were some little buzzing insects,
however, that she did not like at all, and those
were the mosquitoes, which used sometimes
to bite her face, and her arms, and hands,
and make her itch very much; but nurse
never put her to bed at night after she had
found out the tricks of these little creatures
without letting down some nice net curtains
which covered her quite round, so that these
little plagues could not get in.   And in

the day time her little teases were very quiet.

When Rosy used to walk in the Park in London, one of her great pleasures was to run after the sheep and lambs. She never had caught one yet, not even a tiny lamb, though she had run very fast to try **and** stroke some of them, because as soon as she got near they always ran away. Still she hoped that some day or other she should get close up so as to be able to put her arms round the neck of one and hold it tight while she kissed and stroked it.

There were not many sheep near the house, though now and then she met a few in the roads as they were coming home at night; but Cecile had told her that there were a good many in one particular place to which they had never walked. So she begged her mamma to take her out there for a walk one day, and as her kind mamma was quite willing they set off.

The sun was shining very brightly; the sky was very, very blue and clear, and there was a nice, cool air. Altogether it was a most delicious day; and little Rosy, as she trotted by her mamma's side, not in her wooden shoes, but in nice little boots, which were nearly new, chattered away as fast as her small tongue could move.

Her mamma called her a little magpie, but Rosy said,—

'Ma, I can't help it, there is so much to say.' Then she took a little run to the top of a small mound, and called out, 'Oh, mamma, do come here; there is such a funny thing walking about up here. Do come.'

So her mamma got up the mound, too, and when she had looked at what Rosy showed her, she said,—

'Well, my chick, and what is its name?'

'I don't know, mamma, isn't it something like a grasshopper?'

And as Rosy said so she poked the creature with a little bough, and it flew off on to the trunk of a tree, and began to walk up it.

'Oh, mamma,' cried the child, 'I didn't want it to go, I didn't know it could fly. What was its name?'

'Do you remember what they were that came up with an east wind over the land of Egypt, when Moses stretched out his rod because the wicked king Pharaoh would not let the children of Israel go; those creatures that came in such great swarms that they made it quite dark, and ate all the green things and spoilt the harvest? Papa was reading about them yesterday.'

'I know—locusts,' cried Rosy, clapping her hands. 'Do locusts come here?'

'Not the large ones, Rosy, but they say that some do; and I think this is one. Aren't you glad to have seen one?'

'Oh, yes, I am, and I'll tell papa about it. How nice!' And Rosy rubbed her hands again. It was a way she had when she was very pleased. A minute after she cried out, 'There are the sheep, mamma. May I run after them?'

'We will go together, Rosy,' said her mamma.

'What funny sheep they are, mamma; they have got such long legs, haven't they? and such long faces, too?'

'I can see some brown ones out there, Rosy, look! You never saw brown ones before, did you?'

'Oh, how funny! but, mamma, these sheep don't run away. May I go and catch one and bring him to you?'

'We will both go, Rosy,' answered her mamma, again, who was afraid that the sheep might prove too strong for her little girl. 'No, they are not at all afraid. Let us go and talk to that little lamb.'

But while her mamma was pointing to this same lamb, Rosy felt something pulling her from behind. It was something pulling her hat,—her nice new hat, with the pretty leaves and flowers round it which mamma had trimmed so lately, and which Rosy liked so much.

What could it be that was pulling?

K

She put up her right hand to hold it on, and turned her head to see what it could be; and there she saw a great, tall sheep, with long legs, close behind her.

Rosy called out, and then her mamma turned round and gave this rude sheep a great pat with her parasol, which made him let go and run away; but it did not seem frightened one bit, and wanted to come back again and eat the flowers which it evidently took for real ones; so they were obliged to walk very fast to get out of the sheep's way altogether.

And so, you see, poor little Rosy had another disappointment. Perhaps you did not know what that long word meant before; but you can guess now, I think.

She was disappointed about the boots, and now about the sheep; and she did not

'It was something pulling her hat, her nice new hat with the pretty leaves and flowers.'

like her hat to be spoilt either. So at first I am afraid she was inclined to be rather cross and angry with the poor sheep, who could not know as well as Rosy that hats were not meant to eat.

What would you have done if you had been near Rosy then? Wouldn't you have told her that after her beautiful walk and seeing a locust, too, she should not be cross about anything? And wouldn't you have told her that no little child can have every-thing *quite* as she likes; and that any little girl who means to be good must try to be gentle, and kind, and good-tempered, when things happen that she does *not* like, just as much as when everything goes her way?

CHAPTER XIV.

THE WOUNDED BIRD.

BEFORE Rosy got home she found out that she was not the only little creature that sometimes had little troubles. Indeed, I rather fancy that she came to believe that some very small creatures indeed had much larger troubles than she had ever known.

Her mamma and she had nearly got to the garden-gate, and Rosy's little tongue had been silent for some time, when they met a man, who had in his hand a very pretty little bird.

The man came up to Rosy, and said,—

'Would missy care to have this little thing?'

Rosy started with delight, and looked up at her mamma to know what she was to say.

Her mamma did not speak, but went up to look at the bird.

'Why it is a wounded bird!' she said. 'Here are drops of blood. The bird has been shot, and I suppose it will soon die.'

'No, madam,' answered the man; 'it is but little injured, and would soon come round with care. I was about to take it home when I saw your little lady's face, and thought, maybe, she might like to have a pet.'

'What do you say, Rosy?' asked her

mamma. 'There is an empty cage in the kitchen. Shall we take it and let it live there?'

'Oh, mamma, do let it,' cried Rosy, 'and do let it be mine.'

'Well, if you like, my child; but what will you say to this kind gentleman?'

Rosy looked up in his face with her blue eyes, and one of her best smiles, as she said,—

'Thank you, very, very much, sir. Rosy will take great care of the poor little bird.'

Then she held up her frock to make a bed for it, and the man said,—

'It cannot fly yet because it has been hurt, but it will soon be quite well again, and sing you a great many songs, my pretty babe.'

' Would Missy care to have this little thing ?'

Rosy hardly knew what to make of this speech, for though she did not object to be called pretty, she hated of all things to be thought a baby.

However, she supposed that he must mean to be kind, and the thought of the poor bird soon put everything else out of her head.

'What shall we do with it, mamma?' she asked, as soon as he was gone. 'Shall we send for the doctor?'

'Oh, no, I don't think we will do that; papa will be doctor enough, I think; he knows all about birds, you know, Rosy.'

Rosy could quite believe that; and bustling into the room where her papa was sitting, she very soon showed her newly-gotten treasure. Her papa looked at it very carefully, and then said,—

'Well, Rosy, I hope we shall soon get it well;' and then he went to a cupboard and brought out one of the prettiest, softest little nests that you ever saw. 'See, Rosy, isn't it funny? I picked this up to-day and brought it home for you; but I didn't know that you would have a use for it. Now I think it will make a beautifully soft bed for your dickie. Let us put it into the cage, and then put birdie in and give it some sopped bread and water. Cecile can go for some seed afterwards; and perhaps we might put a little bread poultice on to the sore place.'

Rosy thought all these most capital plans, and that there never was anything half so delightful as that dear little nest.

She soon coaxed the poor bird to eat,

but it seemed more glad of the water than of anything else.

Then they put the cage in a sunny place; and when it had been well attended to, they left Rosy to talk to it that it might get fond of its little mistress; and besides, it did not seem to like too much company.

In a very short time Rosy came to tell her mamma that her new pet was beginning to chirp and move about its nest. She was quite sure that by the next day it would be quite cured and able to hop about its cage.

It was a brown bird, with a thick throat, and now Rosy wanted to know its name.

Her mamma said she did not know, but her papa told her that it was a nightingale, and that some day it would sing splendidly.

'It has four different notes, Rosy,' he said, 'and I think it will outdo Mister Tommy. I wonder if they will be good friends.'

'Oh, yes, I'm sure they will,' answered Rosy, ''cause Tommy so likes singing. May they live in one cage, papa?'

'If they like, but I don't much fancy that they will like it,' said her papa. 'I should be rather afraid of their pecking each other's eyes out.'

'But, papa,' cried Rosy, 'my hymn says,—

   '"Birds in their little nests agree."'

'Ah, Rosy,' replied her papa, laughing, 'I think that can be only when they are all of one kind. I never knew a canary and a nightingale to live together in one nest. If you go out and look in the hedges

you will find all sparrows in one nest, not
sparrows and thrushes, and so on; and if
you look up at a rookery you won't find
thrushes among them. But we shall see.
If the canary and the nightingale should become very good friends, we can put them
into one cage and let them play and sing
together. Do you think you can manage
to teach them a tune which they could sing
as a duet; just as mamma and aunt Janie
do?'

'Yes, papa,' said Rosy; 'I know the
Happy Land, and I will try to teach them
that.'

'Do,' said her papa; 'and if you manage it I shall say that you are a capital bird-
trainer.'

After this Rosy climbed on her papa's
knee and began to tell him about the locust

she had seen, and about the sheep which ate part of her hat. And her papa in his turn told her of some much better behaved sheep which he had seen,—sheep that were so good that they did everything their shepherd told them.

'The shepherd was not obliged to go behind them,' he said, 'but he walked in front, and the sheep came after him. He walked faster than they did once, and so they were left a little way behind, but when he called to them they came running up to him just as if they were very fond of him. It made me think, my child, of something which I read to you not long ago out of the Bible. Do you remember who it was that called Himself " the Good Shepherd ?" '

' Jesus Christ,' said Rosy, softly, 'and Jesus Christ was the Son of God.'

' Yes, Rosy ; and who are His sheep ?'

Rosy stopped, and looked puzzled. She had forgotten this ; and at last she said, ' she did not know.'

So her papa said,——

' The sheep are all those people who love Jesus, and listen to His voice and follow Him ; but who are the little lambs in His flock ?'

' Are they the little children ?' asked Rosy, eagerly.

' Yes, Rosy ; all little children who love to hear the words that Jesus spake when He was on earth, those which are written down in the Bible for us, you know, and who try to do as He bids them, are His little lambs. I wonder if Rosy has been trying to please the Good Shepherd this morning.'

Rosy hung down her head, for she re-

membered how cross she had been that
morning, and at last she whispered,—

'Not all the time, dear papa.'

And then she told what she had not told
before, and said she would never be cross
again ; and her papa told her that if she
wanted to be good she must ask Jesus to
help her and teach her how ; and so they
talked on until some one came to see papa,
and their talk ended for that day.

CHAPTER XV.

ROSY HELPS OLD PETER.

WE have forgotten all about Julia for a long time; but it is not because Rosy has left off caring for her. She took her out every day just as she used to do in England, and often told her mamma that she thought the dear dolly was getting a great deal fatter and more rosy every day.

That was because every one used to say this of Rosy herself. A country life agreed with her wonderfully; and she was getting so stout and sturdy that nursey used to tell her that grandmamma would never know her when she went back home again.

There was a time when Rosy was very fond of a drive with mamma, but now she despised carriages altogether, and said that she ' could walk miles and miles !'

There very seldom came a wet day at Cannes, though there was often a windy one ; but that Rosy did not mind. She liked of all things to run in a high wind, and let her hair blow behind her, but it was only in the shade that she was allowed to do so, because in the sun she had to wear her hat, or she would have got a headache.

Rosy had a great many treats during the winter,— for winter out there is not like winter in England. Often it was beautifully fine and warm, and when her little cousins wrote to tell her of the fun they had in playing at snow-balls, she used to get her mamma to write them back messages about the pic-nics she had been to, and the flowers she had picked.

For Rosy could not write yet herself, and her mamma said she could not think of teaching her until she became more industrious over her reading.

You see her mamma was a little bit afraid that her little girl would go back a regular dunce, and that would have been a sad thing.

It is better for boys and girls not to play quite all day, or else they get tired of it; but Rosy was not quite old enough to see that, so she always wanted to go out into the fields, or on the hills, directly after breakfast.

I must say that there was plenty to tempt

L

her, especially when the spring came, and hay-making began. The orange-trees were in blossom then, and they looked prettier than you can imagine, and smelt,—oh, so nice!

Do you know that lots of people have orange-trees on purpose to get plenty of flowers to make that nice stuff called orange-flower water.

Did you ever smell that? Perhaps not; but I must tell you that a great deal of this water is sent to the place where they make that nice 'Eau de Cologne,' which mamma puts on her handkerchief. The orange-flower water helps to make it; and so they pick the flowers instead of letting them turn into fruit.

There is very little grass in Cannes; but some grows out in a plain near; and there, in May, there was to be a grand hay-making, which Rosy was to go and see. 'Ah, and help, too,' so she said, and so she thought. Little girls always like to help; don't they? I am sure you do.

But the grass must be cut before it could be made into hay, and old Peter was to cut a great deal of it. He was a particular friend of Rosy's; and he had promised to let her know the day before he began.

So one evening he paid her a visit, and said, in French,—

'Miss Rosy, I'm a going mowing to-morrow, will you come and help an old man?'

Rosy had learnt a little French by this time, and could talk in her way to old Peter.

So she ran in to ask her mamma.

'I may, mayn't I, dear mamma? Please

say yes, because Peter is very old, and I want to help him.'

'Do you think you can?' asked papa, smiling, 'I'm afraid you could not manage a great scythe.'

'Oh, I don't want one, papa,' cried Rosy, 'I can pick lots with my own hands. Yes, indeed I can, for I picked a great bunch yesterday.'

'Well, if old Peter really wants you, and nurse does not mind the walk, you may have a donkey and go, Rosy,' said her papa, 'and mamma and I will come and see you mowing. Only mind, you must work hard and not chatter too much over it.'

Rosy promised, and then ran off to ask nurse, and to tell old Peter.

'Only I mustn't come if it rains, Peter,' she added, 'but it won't rain; will it?'

She looked at the sky a good deal that night, and asked nurse very often what she thought about the weather; and in the morning, the very first thing she did was to look up in the sky again.

It was as blue as blue could be, and not a cloud anywhere in sight.

Rosy clapped her hands, and her little tongue began its day's work without remembering about the chattering.

Directly after breakfast the donkey came —and a very fine donkey it was, with pink tassels hanging over its face to keep off the flies, and a basket-saddle fit for a little princess. A girl came to drive it; and she wore a very large hat to keep off the sun, and talked very loud and fast to the donkey, just as if it could understand all she said.

Rosy could not, however, because she spoke such funny words.

They soon came to the place where the grass was to be cut.   It was in a flat place, through which ran a pretty winding river, over which was a bridge.   There were mountains at the back of this flat place, or plain, as it was called, and on the tops of those furthest off she could see snow.

Old Peter came up and lifted her off her donkey, and he said that the snow on these mountains never melted, because it was so cold up there, just as her papa had told her.

Then he showed her some vines which were growing on the lower parts of the hills near them, and the orange-trees all covered with white flowers not far off, and asked her if God's world were not a beautiful one?

Rosy thought it was indeed; she was in great spirits that morning, and thought everything nice. So now she ran off so fast to the place where Peter had been at work mowing, that his old legs could scarcely keep up with her little fat ones.

He soon took up his scythe and began his work, cutting down a great many stalks of grass at every stroke. Rosy watched him for a little while to see how he did it, and then she set to work too.

She had no knife, not even a pair of scissors, though she wished she had brought them, but she put out her hand bravely and tugged away at the tall pieces until she had got quite a handful.

It was very good fun at first; but the stalks were so tough, that her little hands soon got tired.

Still she did not give in for a long time. She thought she was really helping, and would not stop only because she was tired.

It was so nice to feel of some use, so Rosy went on till she became quite hot, and old Peter said,—

' Now, missie, it's time for you to leave off, or your good nursey will be giving me a scolding.'

But Rosy answered,—

' My papa is not come yet, and he won't like to see me idle. Why doesn't papa come ?'

Old Peter did not know; but he said,—

' Let us go and ask nurse about it.'

He was rather afraid that the little woman would be ill, that was the truth; and so he led her off to where nurse was sitting at work under a tree.

' She tugged away at the tall pieces until she had got quite a handful.

Nurse was rather afraid too when she saw those red cheeks, and she got up and walked about with her, looking for flowers until they had got paler.

Then papa and mamma came, and they all walked about and talked to Peter; and Rosy picked a few more handfuls and put them among the grass which he had cut. So every one was happy; and every one thought it would make a very pretty hay-field, when the grass was all down and ready to be tossed about.

CHAPTER XVI.

THE RIDE ON THE DONKEY.

ROSY went again to the field the next day with her papa, and found that all the grass was cut, and that Peter, and his son, and some other men, were tossing it over and over, and up into the air on great forked sticks, that it might be turned towards the hot sun on all sides, and so get quite dry.

This was better fun than even seeing it cut, and Rosy had soon begged a little fork that she might toss it about too. But it was very hot where the hay-makers were,—too hot for a little English girl,—and so her papa found an olive-tree near the stream, and under its shade he and Rosy tossed up the grass in grand style.

They came again when it was quite dry and made into hay, and saw Peter's son putting a lot of it on a donkey's back to be carried away.

Now Rosy knew this donkey very well. Its name was Jack, and it was rather a young donkey and a very good one. She had never been on its back, though she had often wished for a ride, because Cecile had told her how well it behaved, and how fond it was of its mother.

She knew its mother too. Her name was Jenny; and when Jack met her out he always used to like to have a little talk with her, only they could not stop long because they were both too busy.

Rosy thought that Jack must like his work in the hay-field very much. He certainly seemed to enjoy the smell of the hay, and kept snuffing it in, and fidgeting as if he thought it would make him a good lunch. But his master only let him have a little taste; he said he had eaten a good breakfast and would make himself ill if he ate any more.

So poor Jacky had to stand quite still and have it put on his back instead.

When he was well loaded, old Peter said,—

' Now would little Missie like to ride on the top? Here's a soft seat and a safe one.'

Rosy had never thought of this before, but now when old Peter asked her she was eager to get up.

'Oh, papa, may I?' she cried. 'Do let me.'

But he said,——

'Rosy, you have never learnt to ride, and you don't know how. What if you were to tumble down!'

'Oh, no, papa, I shouldn't tumble down indeed;—indeed I know how,' she cried pulling his hand. 'I've seen the ladies ride in the Regent's Park; and I saw them in Paris too. Besides, papa, I have been on a rocking-horse,—twice, papa, I have, and I didn't fall off then.'

Papa laughed and said,——

'My little Rosy thinks she can do everything.' And then he took her up in his arms and gave her a great jump and a great swing right on to the top of the hay.

'Oh, papa, how nice!' cried Rosy.

'It's splendid up here. I'm taller than you now, papa, and I can see such a long way; and I couldn't fall, see, papa, for I'm almost buried. Oh, it is so delicious!'

'Well now, Rosy, you must drive your donkey to its home, you know. Do you know what to say?'

'Oh, yes, I know,' said Rosy. 'Gee up, donkey, gee up!' Rosy had a little bough in her hand which was meant to do instead of a stick. It would not reach Mr. Jack's back, but she said he was afraid of it, and thought he had better go before she beat him. Peter's son walked close behind to prevent Rosy from falling off, and perhaps he gave Jacky a push sometimes; but Rosy did not see that.

She thought it was all her doing, and said,——

'See, papa, the donkey does just as I tell him; he doesn't stop at all, and when I told him to go to the gate he went directly. Isn't he a good donkey?'

'Very good, Rosy; and I wonder whether he would mind taking you home before he gets rid of his load of hay. Mamma would like to see you perched up there.'

Old Peter was sure that Jack wouldn't mind at all, and his son was sure too; and Rosy was delighted with the idea; so off they started directly.

They had to get out of the field first, and then along a hot road, and up a hill to the house where they lived; and when they came to the hill Jacky did not seem much to admire it. He went slower and slower, and at last stood still.

Then Rosy called out, —

' Oh, you naughty donkey, go on, go on ; ' and she brandished about her little bough.

But Rosy's papa said, —

' Would not my little girl be tired too, and inclined to stop, if she had to go up this hill with such a load? We must give him time to get his breath.'

So Jacky was very glad of that, and went to the bank at the side of the road to eat some leaves which he saw growing there.

Rosy did not much like waiting, and she was half afraid that the good donkey was going to tip her over his head, but she would not seem frightened.

' Is not Jack stronger than me, papa, then ?' she asked after a little while. ' I thought he was so very strong.'

'Rosy had a little bough in her hand, which was meant to do
instead of a stick.'

'Perhaps he may be; but remember he is not much more than a baby yet, and not nearly so old as Rosy.'

'Oh, papa, and how wise he is!' cried Rosy. 'Don't you think he knows a great great deal?'

'I don't suppose he is learning to read,' replied her papa; 'but I shouldn't wonder if he tries to do all a donkey's lessons as well as he can. But who is this coming down the hill to meet us?'

'Mamma! mamma!' screamed Rosy. 'Look, mamma, where I am!'

'I see, my darling, but take care you don't fall off,' answered mamma, looking a little anxious; and then she asked papa whether the child were quite safe.

'Oh, yes, I think so, if she sits very still. She has been enjoying her ride very much,

M

and taking a few lessons from the donkey. And after all this pleasure I hope our little Rosy will be as ready for lessons to-morrow as no doubt the donkey will be for his work. When she can read some litttle stories about donkeys I think I know of a pretty book that she will like; and when she can count up a hundred shells without making a mis-take, I am going to give her a little box to put all in that she can pick up on the beach.'

CHAPTER XVII.

CARRYING THE HAY.

THE good Jack could not carry all the hay that day. He only took a little just to show them how they were getting on up at the farm.

Rosy knew that there was plenty more to do: and she was not at all tired of the hay-field: so she tried very hard to learn some new words at her reading lesson, and to say all that she knew without spelling. After that came the counting; and Rosy's mamma was surprised to find that she could count up to thirty quite well, and that on this day she remembered that two and two make four, three and three six, and four and four eight, without having to find out on her fingers. So she taught her a little more that she had not learned before; and then all the books and the slate were put away, and Rosy stood up before her mamma to say the text which she learnt yesterday, and to learn a new one.

It was only a tiny text that Rosy ever learnt, because she was a tiny girl; but her kind mamma was very glad when she had not forgotten the last one.

She could say quite well, —

'The Lord is my shepherd, I shall not want.'

So now she learnt, —

'He maketh me to lie down in green pastures.'

When she had said it over a few times she knew it, because her mamma had explained to her first what the green pastures were, and told her to think of the nice fields where the hay was made, before the grass had grown long, and when the sheep used to lie in it; and she told her that it meant that God was kind to His people, and took care of them as the shepherd does of his sheep.

Rosy listened, and said that she had asked God to make her one of His little lambs, and to take care of her like that, and asked whether her mamma thought He could hear such a little girl's voice. And her mamma said,—

' Oh, yes, because the good God is always near you, and He loves to hear the little children pray. He can hear my

Rosy even when she does not speak out loud.'

Then Rosy said that she had asked God to make her a good girl that morning, and she said, 'Have I been good, mamma?'

And her mamma kissed her and said,—

'Yes, my Rosy has been a very good girl to-day.'

Then Rosy whispered,—

'May I go again to the field, dear mamma?'

Her mamma did not answer directly, but held up her little girl's chin and looked into her eyes. Then she asked,—

'Was that the reason why Rosy wanted to be good?' and she looked rather disappointed.

But Rosy said very earnestly,—

'Mamma, I did want to be good *really*,

I often do; and I want to go to the hay-field too.'

So her mamma answered,—

'Well, my chicken, you may go; and I will go with you to-day.'

Little Rosy did not stop for more, but ran off and said,—

'Please, nurse, dress me.'

She was soon ready and trotting off by her mamma's side.

Susan, the farmer's daughter, met them at the gate, and catching the little one up in her arms, ran off with her, saying that her cheeks looked like rosy apples, and that she really must let her eat a piece of them.

Rosy knew that was only fun, and she laughed and said,—

'Oh, no, I can't spare any, I want them all myself.'

Then she scrambled down to run up to the waggon which was being laden, and Susan called out that her two legs were just like two stone pillars, they were so firm and strong.

That was exactly what the little girl liked; for of all things she wanted to be very strong. The waggon was already getting very full; and all the people with their large wooden rakes were raking the hay together, and then the men with their great forks hoisted it up and piled it on the top of the heap.

There were two men up on the top too, who were busy laying it all straight, and when the waggon was ready to start they wanted to lift Rosy up; but she said,—

'Oh, no; it is so heavy now for the poor horses, and I am *so* heavy, you know. It wouldn't be kind; they couldn't draw me at all.'

The truth was, perhaps, that Rosy was a little bit afraid of getting up so high, and then old Peter was not on the top, but some strange men that she did not know. So she ran to her mamma's side and said,—

'I had better not go up, mamma; had I?'

And her mamma thought not; so Rosy got some one to lend her the great whip, and she ran as fast as her little legs would carry her after the horses, and pretended to beat them.

That was only fun; for the poor horses were very good, and pulled away as hard as they could. Rosy would not have beaten them for the world; and I don't much think that the men would have let her go near enough; for perhaps the horses might not have liked to be struck by such a little girl. They might have been offended and kicked; and then poor little Rosy might have got knocked down and hurt very much.

So Rosy only ran near the waggon and cried out,—

'Gee up, Mister Light Horse; gee up Mister Red Horse; or else Rosy will get to the gate first.'

And all the people shouted when the waggon started, and said something which meant 'Hurrah;' and it looked very pretty going under the olive-trees, and through the meadows, out into the open road, and so to the farm.

That hay-making was a very pleasant time, and Rosy said that she had never been so happy in all her life, and that she never

'Gee up, Mr. Light Horse! Gee up, Mr. Red Horse!'

should forget it,— not even if she lived to be a hundred years old.

It was a pleasant time, too, for her papa and mamma and nursey, because their little Rosy tried hard to be very good,—not to be cross or rude or selfish or unkind all the time; but kind and gentle and polite to every one. And two or three times when she was beginning to snatch her hat or her stick from nurse when she was helping her, she all at once remembered and said,—

'I so sorry, nurse; please kiss Rosy.'

CHAPTER XVIII.

THE BEGINNING OF A SAD ADVENTURE.

SOME time after the haymaking Rosy's papa and mamma went out one day to pay some visits. They left Rosy with nurse and told her to be very good, and only to play in the garden or in the little field which was near the houses. She was to do everything that nurse told her, and not tease her a bit, or ask for a walk, because the good nursey had a head-ache.

Rosy did not much like being left at home, for lately she had gone out so often with her papa and mamma that she thought she should be very dull, especially as her nurse was so poorly. However, she promised; and she quite intended to be the best of little girls that day.

As soon as they had done their breakfast, and her papa and mamma were gone, they went into a sitting-room, which opened into the garden.

The sun was very hot, and nursey's head ached so much that she could not go out at all. She would have liked Rosy to stay in-doors, and play with her doll for a little while, because then she would not have been obliged to keep getting up to see where her chicken was.

But Rosy did not like staying in even for a little while; so the kind nurse did not say no, but let her run out before the window, only she bid her keep in sight.

For some time the child sat on a little seat making a daisy-chain for herself, which she brought in pretty often to show how it was getting on.

When that was done she crept under the orange-trees and began picking several kinds of large wild flowers, which she knew she might have. These were intended as a present for her dear mamma when she came home, and it took a little time to make them up into a nosegay quite to her mind.

When that was done she went in again to show this grand present to her nursey.

But poor nurse was lying down then, and half asleep. She only said,—

'Yes, dear. I'll look by-and-by. Mind you keep quite in sight, and don't put anything into your mouth.'

And Rosy, seeing that it teased her to talk to her, went out again in search of some way of amusing herself.

There were no oranges now on the trees to tempt her, for they had all been gathered to make marmalade. When they were being picked Rosy had one to taste, but she did not much like it, for it was so bitter. Now these same trees were getting covered with white blossoms again, and Rosy liked the smell, and sometimes wished she might have some; but they were a great deal too high for her to reach.

So she went round and round the garden, and into the first little field, picking wild flowers and watching the bees and flies and other insects that settled on them. It was a dull time certainly for the poor little girl, for she had no one to play with.

Perhaps you may wonder why she did not fetch Julia, and play with her in-doors; but unfortunately that young lady had had a dreadful fall and broken her nose. It had therefore been thought the best plan to send her to a doll-doctor, to get a new head and neck. So, you see, poor little Rosy was left quite alone.

I think that the best way for her would have been to stay by poor nursey's side and build a house with her bricks quite quietly; but Rosy did not think so.

She wandered about until she saw, in one part, a little hole in the hedge which she had never noticed before, and through this hole a bunch of beautiful scarlet ane-mones pushing themselves into the garden.

Rosy loved anemones, and when she peeped down she saw that there were much better ones on the other side. The hole was large enough for her to creep through, and through she went in a minute. There were some other sweet smelling flowers there as well, and soon she had picked a good many, and was just going back with them, when suddenly a most magnificent butterfly took a fancy to her flowers, and settled on her bunch.

Rosy laughed out loud with pleasure, but she did not touch it for fear of hurting it, only she stood still to admire it.

But the butterfly would not stay to be looked at; it saw some violets further on, and flew to get sweets out of them. Rosy ran, too, for she also liked violets, and she thought to pick the very one on which it had settled. However, the butterfly was too quick for her. It had seen a buttercup

N

further on, and away it went in an instant. Rosy was as quick in following, and so they continued their game until she suddenly found herself on the bank of the river.

The butterfly flew across, which was not at all fair of it, as little girls have no wings, and so Rosy could not cross too. But she did not think of that. It was the re-collection of what she had done that she thought of now.

What had her mamma said to her about keeping close to the house, and about never going near water? And what had she pro-mised?

Rosy was all at once filled with shame and fear; for besides being sure that she had done wrong she remembered what her papa had told her about little children who will not keep near their nurses, sometimes falling into the hands of wicked people, and never seeing their dear mammas again.

She turned to go home, but she had run so far that now she could not see the gate or the hedge through which she had crept.

She ran a little one way, then another, then stood still and felt inclined to cry or even to scream for help.

Just at this moment she spied a man fishing in the river with a long line.

At first she was frightened, and thought perhaps he was a wicked man and might do her some harm; when at the same moment the man also turned and saw her.

He lifted his line out of the water, and while he was putting some fresh bait on the hook, he began to ask her if she did not belong to the lady who was staying at that large house up yonder. He told her also

that she was a pretty little girl, and just the
very image of her mamma.

Rosy was pleased at this, and thought
that he must be a nice man, as he knew her
mamma and spoke so politely to herself.
She did not mind being told she was pretty
at all; and besides she was very anxious to
watch some one fishing. She had never
seen fishes caught before, only pictures of
such things. So now she stood by and
saw the man put the bait on the hook to
make the fishes come, and then throw the
line into the water. The man told her not
to speak or she would frighten the fishes
away, but to watch the end of the line.
Very soon she saw the water move. A
fish had come to eat the worm on the hook
and tugged the line down; but the man
who held the rod fast, pulled it out quickly,

'The man pulled it out quickly, and there was a fish at the end of it.'

and there was a fish at the end of it, with the hook sticking in its mouth, wriggling on the bank.

Rosy did not like to see it so much hurt; and she was glad when the man took it off the hook. But even then it lay gasping for breath; and Rosy remembered that her mamma had told her that fishes could not breathe out of water; and she cried out,—

'Oh, please put it in again.'

But the fisherman said,—

'Oh, no, we want to eat it. Do you never eat fish?'

Rosy certainly did, for she was very fond of them; but still she thought it a great pity that taking them out of the water prevented them from living.

CHAPTER XIX.

FALL INTO THE RIVER.

ROSY was so taken up with the fishing now that she had quite forgotten about her having done just what her mamma had said she must not do, in running down to the water. She had forgotten her fears, too, about what nurse would say, and also about this fisherman, whether he might not be intending to run away with her as well as the fish; she only thought about the poor dying fish, and was making up her mind never to eat fish again, when the man put the fishing-rod into her hand and bid her try to catch one herself.

She was afraid to say no, though her little heart beat fast, and besides the fishing-rod was so very heavy that she could hardly hold it. I think that fisherman could not have known much about little children, or he would never have put such a great thing into her hand.

Poor Rosy hoped that no fishes would come, and would have liked to call to them to keep away, but the fisherman put his finger on her mouth, and whispered,—

'Keep very still.'

She was afraid to disobey; and at that very moment a fish pulled at her hook.

Then the man called out,—

'Pull in, pull in quick!'

And poor Rosy tried; but the fish was a large one, and it could pull too. It had no idea of being caught by such a little

child and thought it would catch her instead.

Poor little Rosy was frightened then indeed. She tugged away in her turn; but
it was of no use, the fish was the stronger
of the two; and in another moment her
little feet had slipped from under her, and
down she fell into the river.

How do you think she felt as she went
splash in? I am sure I cannot tell you;
but I dare say lots of things came into her
little head all at once; but it was time for
the fisherman to be frightened then as well
as Rosy.

He was not used to small children and
did not know that a big fish might prove as
strong as a little girl, so he had never thought
of her being pulled in. But as soon as he
saw her fall down the bank, after her he

'The fish had no idea of being caught by such a small child, and thought it would catch her instead.'

sprang, and before she had gone quite under the water he had got hold of a bunch of her clothes, and pulled her out again. She had never let go the fishing-rod, but held it more tightly as she fell; it was something to cling to; so at the same time that he fished out Rosy he pulled out a great fish also.

Poor Rosy was pale and trembling, for she had thought she was going to be drowned; she was wet and cold besides, and instead of saying, 'thank you,' to the man, for getting her out, she only felt cross with him for having made her fish when she did not want to do anything of the kind.

That was because she was cross with herself, you know, and because she remembered now how bad it was of her to run out of the garden, and all that long way from

home, when her mamma had told her to
keep near it and nurse.

The fisherman said to her,——

' Never mind, missie.   It's all right.'

But she thought,——

' No, it isn't ; it's all wrong.'

CHAPTER XX.

THE WOUNDED HAND.

THE man saw that Rosy looked very pale and frightened; so he tried to amuse her by showing her the great fish she had caught.

'Look what a splendid fellow we've got; why it was worth a ducking to catch such a one!'

But Rosy did not care to look at the fish, though she certainly did not feel so sorry for this one as for the other, because she was cross with it for dragging her into the water so rudely.

It was an enormous carp, and weighed at least six pounds; and as it lay panting on the bank Rosy thought it must at least be a whale; and she shuddered to look at it.

But she was obliged to look for all that, for the man was delighted with his prize, and kept showing her its eyes, its head, and its back, until Rosy said at last in despair,—

'I want to go home; I so cold,' and began to cry.

Then the fisherman was very sorry, and took Rosy up in his arms to comfort her. But when he had lifted her up he saw that her little hand was bleeding. She had bruised and torn it against the stones on the bank of the river when the fish pulled her in.

So the man bathed the poor little hand in the clear, cool water, and tied Rosy's little handkerchief round it. Then he shouted as loud as he could, to see if any one was near who would take Rosy home while he went to fetch the doctor. And soon a boy and a girl came running up, who lived at the farm where Rosy went to see the dairy, and who knew Rosy very well.

The man told them how she had been hurt, and they promised to take her home very quickly. And the man gave the boy the great fish to carry for Rosy, and said he would send the doctor directly.

So they set off to run home; for Rosy was very wet and cold, and very unhappy. The boy kept showing her the fine fish, but she did not care about it at all, and only wished it back again in the water.

When they got home Cecile opened the door, and was very much surprised to see Rosy in such a state; but when she heard what had happened, she thanked the boy and girl for bringing her home, and said that nurse had gone to sleep, but she would take care of Rosy till the doctor came.

So Cecile undressed her directly, and when she had been well rubbed with warm flannels and was laid down in bed, she was obliged to tell her tale; and I will say that she told it all quite truly, and did not even lay the blame on the butterfly. Only she said she did not think she was going so far away, and meant to come back in a minute.

Her hand which had got scratched and torn in her fall down the bank began to be very painful. It smarted a great deal; and

' Rosy did not care anything about the fish ; she only wished it back
again in the water.'

she wondered what the doctor would do to it. She thought that doctors always hurt people a great deal before they cure them; and she was afraid even of nurse touching her hand.

Then he would be a strange doctor too, and Rosy never liked strangers; so her heart went pit-a-pat.

Besides this there was the thought of her dear papa and mamma. They would be coming back soon, and what would they say? and what would nurse say? Oh, how she did wish that she had never disobeyed them!

Cecile did not say much, for she saw that the little girl was punished enough; but Rosy knew what she must think of her, and almost felt as if it would be better if she would scold.

Then Cecile told her that the doctor lived a great way off, and could not come yet; and that papa and mamma were not coming home for several hours; so she said she should have some hot broth for dinner and then go to sleep.

Cecile thought that the broth would be better than meat just then, and that it would warm the child; but Rosy did not like broth, she would rather have had meat or pudding. She was going to say so when the thought came into her head that perhaps it was because she had not been good; so she drank the broth and said nothing.

She lay down as Cecile bid her and tried to keep her eyes shut; but it was early to go to bed, and Rosy was not sleepy. At any other time she would have asked Cecile to tell her stories or to sing to her; but now she did not dare because she was so ashamed.

She got hot, and tossed about in spite of trying to keep quiet; and poor Cecile, who knew that little children sometimes become very ill after such accidents, was very uneasy. She watched her anxiously; but she did not say what she was thinking about.

At last Rosy's eyelids became very heavy, and, to Cecile's great joy, she fell asleep. The hot, feverish look went away by degrees, and her little face and hands grew moist. So the good French maid lifted up her heart, and thanked God that the darling child had not been drowned, and prayed that she might not have any illness.

Do you think that Rosy dreamed at all while she was asleep?

O

I think she did, and that they were not pleasant dreams, because she started two or three times, and once threw out her arms and gave a low cry.

When she did so, kind Cecile put her hand on her shoulder, and patted her gently, and then she lay still again and slept quietly. Perhaps that finished one dream; but I think she began another each time.

What funny things dreams are! And sometimes we dream about things that we don't care about one bit. But any one could see that it was not so with Rosy then.

She told them to her nurse afterwards; and so I can tell them to you. First she thought she was a little tiny fish swimming about very happily in the river, with the sun shining overhead, and feeling very cool and comfortable in the water, when up came a large, large fish with a great head and a tail like no fishes that she had ever seen. It was more like that of the great sow with the fifteen young ones, which she had often seen since that day when she carried the pears to them. This great fish was very fierce, she thought; and it wanted to eat her; so she gave that scream, and then nurse came and took her out of the water. She forgot in her dream, you see, that fishes do not have nurses.

Then she slept again, and dreamt that she had been running very fast in the garden, and had tumbled down and hurt her knees. It pained her very much, and her mamma said that it was all her own fault, for that she ought not to have run so fast.

It was not like her dear mamma to say

so, and Rosy thought it was very unkind. Then some one came and said,—

'The doctor is coming, and he will be sure to put a leech on to the place.'

She knew what leeches were, because once she had seen them put on her papa's head when he had a headache; and she knew that they bit people, and it made her very frightened; and she was very unhappy and began to cry, thinking that every one seemed to be so unkind and so different to what they used to be.

How delightful it was to wake and find only Cecile sitting by her, and looking at her kindly, and to hear her say that now if Rosy felt quite well she might be dressed in dry clothes and get ready to see the doctor!

The little girl could not help putting

her arms round Cecile's neck, and giving her a great many kisses, though she still felt too much ashamed to talk as she used to do.

In a little while these ugly dreams were almost forgotten, only she still felt even more afraid of the doctor than she had been before she went to sleep, and had a sort of idea that he would do something very dreadful to that poor little smarting hand of hers.

CHAPTER XXI.

THE DOCTOR'S VISIT.

BUT Rosy was not allowed to jump out of bed and sit on the floor to put on her shoes and socks as she was used to do, for fear she should catch cold. She was obliged to have them put on in bed while she was covered up all but her feet. And then she had to be washed in warm water, and rubbed for rather a long time, and after that to be dressed quickly on Cecile's lap for fear she should get any cold.

She did not like this a bit. What she

liked was to fly about like a little madcap, and help to dress herself.

But then it was all her own fault, you know; so Rosy could not complain.

The last string of her pinafore was not tied before there came a loud rat, tat, tat, at the door, and Rosy's little heart began to beat as if it wanted to get through her side, while her two cheeks grew first red and then very pale.

She did not *know* that it was the doctor. It might be a visitor, of course; but Cecile said,—

' I wonder who that can be !'

And Rosy said that she thought she could guess. It could not be her papa and mamma, she knew; for they never knocked or rang, but just walked straight in at a little door which was always open; and if it

could have been them, poor Rosy's heart
would not have been very quiet, because of
that dreadful tale that would have to be
told.

But she had not to wait very long.

In less than two minutes up came one
of the servants to say that the doctor was
come, and wanted to see Miss Rosy directly.

'Oh, dear,' sighed Rosy, 'but you'll
come, too, won't you, Cecy?'

She always said 'Cecy' when she wanted
to coax; and now she put the hand that
was well into Cecile's, and drew her along.

When they got to the room-door Cecile
said,—

'Now, Miss Rosy, you must go in first,'
and she let go her hand to open the door.

Poor Rosy went in looking very red;

but she kept both her hands under the pinafore, and hung down her head.

The doctor spoke to her, but she answered so low that he could not hear a word; so Cecile came and sat down by her, and pulled her to her knee, and said,—

'Come, Miss Rosy, dear, you must show the gentleman your hand.'

Then Rosy took courage, and lifted up her head to have a good look at the doctor.

He was an old gentleman, and wore gold spectacles on his nose. He did not look at all cruel or unkind; but still Rosy was frightened, and hid her face again in Cecile's lap.

What was it that made her so much more afraid now than she was of the strange man by the river when she was all alone?

She was a little afraid of him; but then she had only begun to think that she had done something wrong. Now she *knew* it, and had been thinking about it for a good while.

And people who know that they have been doing wrong are always easily frightened.

At last the good old gentleman said,—

'Come, Miss Rosy, take that little hand from under the pinafore, and put it into mine quite open, so that I may see what is the matter. Doctors can't cure wounds without seeing them, you know.'

Then Rosy all on a sudden took both her hands from under the pinafore. She put one under Cecile's apron, and gave the other to the good doctor.

But which do you think she gave him?

' The good doctor took the little hand, and turned it over and over.'

Not the sick hand, but the well one; for a thought had come into her mind, and she said to herself,——

'The doctor does not know which it is that is hurt, and he won't be able to find anything the matter with this one.'

She did not say a word to him; so when she did it, she did not remember that it was the same thing as telling a lie.

And Cecile said nothing, though she knew it was the wrong hand, for she waited to see what the doctor would say.

CHAPTER XXII.

ROSY TRIES TO DECEIVE THE DOCTOR.

THE good doctor said nothing for a minute. He only took the little hand, and turned it over and over, looked at the back, the palm, and then at each one of the fingers.

It was fat, and white, and perfectly well. One would think that it had never had a scratch in its little life.

'Well, this is very strange,' said the doctor, at last, 'I thought that I was sent for to cure a little wounded hand. They told me that it was all torn and bleeding;

but I can see nothing the matter with it. Has the hand cured itself without my help, or is the mischief inside I wonder? Well, it will be the best plan at any rate to bind it up in this nice bandage until to-morrow that it may rest and get quite well; and meantime, little Miss Rosy must make one hand do to eat with, and to play at her games with. I suppose she can hold dolly in one hand, or is she too large a baby? If so, perhaps nurse will be good enough to take care of her just for one day.'

So saying, the old gentleman went to the table, and took a great many things out of his pockets. He did it slowly, laying one thing down after another, and Rosy meantime stood trembling by Cecile. She wondered that she said nothing and that she still kept that little injured hand quietly in her lap; but Cecile had her own reason for keeping silent.

At last the doctor found just what he wanted, a nice long piece of fine bandaging stuff; and with a very grave face he came back and began slowly to bind up Rosy's hand.

At first he only went round and round the middle of it; so that she could still move the fingers very easily. She did not mind this, and thought that her trick had succeeded; but after two or three turns he began to bind up the fingers too, carefully and gravely, without saying a word or smiling the least bit in the world, until at last she could not stir either finger or thumb, and her hand was of no use at all. Then she began to see what a mistake she had made, and how, while she had been trying to deceive the doctor, she had been caught herself.

' At last she could not stir either finger or thumb.'

She saw that this would never do, and could not bear to think that she could not play at all until the next day; so taking her right hand from out of its hiding-place, and getting very red, she said,—

'Rosy has made a mistake; this hand is quite well, it is the other which was hurt.'

'Oh, what a good thing that we have found out the mistake in time!' cried the old gentleman; 'why if we hadn't, poor little Rosy would have had no hand at all to use, and what a thing that would be?'

And the old doctor looked at Cecile and laughed. He had known quite well all the time how it was.

But Cecile did not laugh nor even smile. She looked quite grave, but she did not speak at all.

The bandage was very soon pulled off

the left hand and rolled up again that it might be quite smooth for the right hand. When the good doctor had looked at the place that was hurt, he said,—

'Dear me! I am afraid that this would have been very bad by to-morrow if it had not been fastened up. I knew a little boy once who had just such a sore place; and he would not have anything done to it for a good while, because he was afraid that every one would hurt him dreadfully who tried to touch it, and what do you think happened?'

Rosy looked curious, and said,—

'What?'

'Why, it got very sore indeed, and smarted so that he cried with the pain, and at last a great swelling came up which had a lot of thick white stuff inside, and that hurt him just as if he had been burnt. So the dreadful old doctor who is so cruel, you know, was obliged to be sent for, and he could do nothing until he had made a hole with this sharp little knife, and let the white stuff run out. Then it got better.'

' But didn't it hurt him dreadfully?' asked Rosy, shuddering.

' Oh, a little, I dare say,' said the doctor, shrugging his shoulders; ' but it was his own fault, you know. It wouldn't have hurt him to have some of this nice salve put on which I am going to put on little Rosy's hand' (and as he spoke he put some nice cool pink stuff on the sore place); ' and it wouldn't have hurt him to have it bound up nicely, as I am going to bind hers, so, you see, he was a silly boy, and we need not pity him much.'

P

CHAPTER XXIII.

THE CONFESSION.

WHEN the good doctor took up the long soft bandage again, and wrapped it very gently and tenderly round the wounded hand, and said,—

'Now does this feel comfortable, Miss Rosy?'

Rosy said it did. She was very glad now that she had had it done; for since the salve was put on it had left off smarting. And she began to think to herself that she had been very much like that foolish little boy. But it had not come into her head

' Now does this feel comfortable, Miss Rosy ? '

that the good doctor had known of her trick all the while, or she would have been much more ashamed of herself than she was.

'My hand feels so much better now, Cecile,' she said, stroking the one which was bound up with the one which was well and free. 'When will it be quite well? And when may I have this taken off?'

But Cecile only looked steadily into Rosy's eyes, and said more gravely than ever,——

'I don't know.'

It made Rosy uncomfortable to feel Cecile looking at her in that way, and she could not make out why she did not get up and take her out of the room.

The doctor, too, was a very long time putting away all his things; and this puzzled her also, for she had often heard that doctors were always very busy, and when her own mamma was ill in London the doctor never stayed many minutes.

At last he said,—

' Well, young lady, I shall come again to - morrow to see how you are getting on.'

And taking up his hat and cane he wished them both good morning.

Hardly had the kind doctor gone, when nurse came into the room. Her long sleep had taken away the bad headache, and now she was very frightened about Rosy, and wondered to see her poor little hand all bandaged up. How sorry she was to hear all the sad story; and then as soon as it was told, the house-door opened, and Rosy's papa and mamma came in.

They knew nothing about what had happened, and her papa was calling out,—

'Rosy, Rosy, come and see the treasures which we have brought you.'

They came into the room, but no Rosy was visible; for at the sound of their voice she had crept behind her nurse, and could not be seen.

'Why, how is this? Is Rosy hiding?' asked mamma.

And nurse was obliged to draw her forward, and Cecile told all the story about the river.

Oh, dear, how hot and red, and then how cold and pale, poor Rosy got, as Cecile told everything.

It would take a long time to tell you how sorry poor mamma was when she heard how her little girl had forgotten all she had said, and all her promises, and how grave papa looked too.

But Cecile told how much she had already suffered, and nurse begged so hard that she might be forgiven this time, and Rosy cried so much, and kissed her papa and mamma so many times, and promised so often ' never, never to do such a naughty thing again,' that at last they both kissed her, and said that as nurse had forgiven her for giving her such a fright, they would forgive her too.

And so that sad day ended with a happier evening than Rosy could have expected. Indeed, her mamma was so very thankful that her dear child had not been drowned, as she might have been, that many times Rosy found that she was looking at her with the tears in her eyes. And so she knew that although she was very sorry to think how little her Rosy could be trusted, yet that she still loved her as dearly as ever. And Rosy made up her mind, never, never again to make any one so unhappy if she could help it.

Nurse had to teach Rosy her new text that night; for her mamma was too tired to go and see her in bed. So she made her say it before she was undressed, and then asked her if she had not a great many things to put into her evening prayer. The little girl knew what that meant very well, for she often had to stand and think before she knelt down. And she soon said that she must thank her great Father up in heaven for not having let her be drowned, and ask Him to forgive her for the naughty thing that she had done.

Then nurse said,—

'Rosy, my child, there is one naughty thing which you did which made me very, very sorry. I have been wondering whether you would find it out; but I don't think you have; so now think.'

Rosy thought a long time, and tried a good many things; but she did not hit on the right, until nurse said,—

'It was something which you did to the doctor.' Now I don't know whether this had come into Rosy's head before; but she certainly got very red when nurse said that, and when she added, 'You told him a story.'

But she *seemed* as if she were quite surprised, and answered,—

'I only *gave* him the wrong hand. I didn't *say* that one was hurt.'

'It was all the same thing, Rosy,' replied her nurse; 'you *did* a story instead of *saying* one. It was very wicked of you.'

'But I didn't *know* it was naughty,' persisted Rosy.

'Was it true then to say that you had *made a mistake?*'

Rosy could not say it was, and she got redder and redder afterwards, and then a few tears began to fall; and at last she said softly,—

'Rosy's a very naughty girl. Rosy's always doing *bads.*'

'Rosy has got a naughty heart,' said nurse, tenderly; 'and she must ask God to give her a new one, or else she never can be a good little girl.'

And then she made her kneel, and Rosy

added some little words of her own to her evening prayer.

Afterwards she got up and wiped her eyes, and nurse laid her in bed and kissed her, and tucked her up just as she always did.   And she was soon asleep.

Rosy was very quiet next morning while she was being dressed.   She seemed to have something in her little mind which would not come out.

It was not until the breakfast-bell rang that she managed it, and then in a great hurry she ran up to her nurse, and whispered,—

'Must I tell Mr. Doctor what a naughty thing I did?'

'Yes; I think you ought,' said nurse.

'Then I will,' said Rosy, in a resolute manner, and down to breakfast she ran.

The doctor came as he had said he would, and nurse brought Rosy down and stayed while the little hand was being dressed again. But her mamma was in the room too, sitting by the window.

The little girl was very quiet while it was being done, and did not speak, though she coughed a great many times; and yet Rosy had no cough.

It seemed very hard to make her little confession; and nurse was afraid that it was never coming; but when Rosy had made up her mind, she was generally pretty determined about doing anything.

The doctor had finished his work, and had said good morning to her mamma, however, and he had turned to go before she spoke. Then all at once, plucking up her courage, she ran after him, and catching hold of the tail of his coat, she said,—

'Rosy was very naughty yesterday, Mr. Doctor. She knew quite well which was the bad hand; and Rosy's very sorry.'

You would have liked to see how the kind old gentleman smiled then, and how pleased he was to see that she had found out her fault. But Rosy's mamma could not make it out at all; so he had to explain what it all meant. And then he had to talk to the little girl about its being a dreadful thing to tell stories or to *deceive* any one, and how surprised he was that such a little girl could have done such a thing. And afterwards he forgave her, and kissed her, and went away.

At dinner that day they had the carp which Rosy had caught. Every one liked it except its little catcher; but the sight of it put too many sad thoughts into her mind for her to be able to enjoy it.

She thought that it had more ' thorns ' in it, as she called the bones, than any other fish, and was very glad when her papa offered to eat her piece as well as his own.

They were to have gone in a boat that day to visit some very pretty little islands which were only a little way off across the sea, and which Rosy had looked at a great many times when she stood on the beach; but it was thought better now to wait a few days; and so Rosy went out for a walk with her papa after dinner.

She took her basket with her because they were going to the beach. And she soon found lots of pretty shells. There were some the shape of snail shells, of very nice colours, large ones and little ones;

and there were some little lilac and white shells which she found in pairs; those were her favourites, and whenever she found a nice pair she was in great glee, and jumped about for joy. Rosy did not get much sea-weed, but she picked up beautiful pieces of coloured rock, some of which had lots of little sparkles in them.

She was very busy filling her basket quietly, while her papa was looking through his long telescope at a ship which was a long way off, when suddenly he cried out,—

' Here, Rosy, make haste, see what there is yonder !'

Rosy jumped up, and then her papa lifted her in his arms, and pointed to some great black thing in the water.

First there seemed to come up a tail, then a head or a leg, she did not know which, but whatever it was, it was having a good game, for it tumbled about, as if it were enjoying itself wonderfully.

'What is it, papa?' said Rosy, after she had looked at it for some time.

'A porpoise, Rosy; there, you never saw one of those before.'

'Oh, what fun!' cried Rosy, clapping her hands; 'how I should like to play with it!'

'It would make a funny pet,' answered her papa, 'and I think you would find it rather strong if you had it in your lap. What would you say if it flapped that great tail in your eyes?'

Rosy laughed very loud at the thought of this, and said,—

'Oh, it would be such fun! Won't you catch it for me, papa?'

'How?' asked her papa, laughing. 'Am I to go wading into the water all that way and draw it out whether it likes it or not? I'm afraid I should soon get out of my depth; and how would you like me to be drowned?'

'Oh, papa,' cried Rosy, 'you know you can swim; you said so, papa.'

'Can I? but I don't think I can try to-day, because the sea is so rough, and besides I should have to go home in wet clothes. What would mamma say if she saw me coming in dripping wet, and with a great porpoise in my arms?'

Rosy thought notwithstanding that it would be 'great fun;' and she was quite disappointed when the porpoise disappeared, and she had to give up all hopes of this strange pet.

CHAPTER XXIV.

GOING HOME AGAIN.

SIX months had now passed since Rosy Girard, and her papa and mamma and nurse, came to stay on the shore of that great sea which has such a long name that I have been quite afraid to tell it to you. It is the same sea which reaches up to the country which we read about in the Bible, and its name is the " Mediterranean."

Rosy had become fonder of looking at its blue waters every day; and her papa told her that perhaps she would never see such a blue sea again.

Q

She had been on it in a boat several times; and sometimes the boat had been moved by oars, and at other times by a sail. She liked to see the men put up the sail very much; and she liked to see the wind fill it, and carry the boat along very fast; only sometimes it rocked up and down very much, and then it made her just a little sick.

They went to the islands one day, and had their dinners out of doors in a lovely woody place. That was a happy day!

But all these pleasures were coming to an end now, for it was getting time to go home again.

Now little people of Rosy's age like changes very much indeed. We all know that. So when mamma and nurse began to talk to the little girl about going home again to see dear grandmamma and aunts and cousins, and the cat, and Tommy, the canary, and the rose-tree, and everything else that she liked, she was not at all sorry; only there were a good many things that she wanted very much to take with her.

The nightingale was quite well and flourishing. He had been cured, oh, a long while ago; and he sang even 'more beau'fully than Tommy.' Of course, he was going with her.

The Dutch dolls, too, had all been dressed, one as an old market-woman in a cap, another with a great wide flapping hat over the cap; one as a young woman riding on a donkey between two panniers, another as a servant girl with a band of black velvet round her head. There were two or three soldiers too, and some children; indeed, all the twelve dollies were dressed differently. They were fixed upon a piece of wood, and Rosy looked at them most days. Of course these had to go, besides her box of shells, some flower-roots for her garden, and a good many other little things. So packing was really an important business; and as the time drew near, the little woman was very busy.

She was quite as fat as when she first came; indeed a good deal fatter, but then she was taller too, and had more rosy cheeks.

She could read, too, a great deal better; for of late she really had settled very nicely every day to her lessons for a little while; and she could make little words with her nice ivory letters, and say a great many little hymns and texts. So, because she had taken pains her kind mamma had begun to teach her to write, and that was just what she had been longing to do for a very long time.

It had been a good deal of trouble certainly to manage all this; but now it was so nice to think of going back to show grand-mamma that she had really learnt 'much, much,' as she promised to do, instead of going back quite a dunce.

And this was a pleasant part of going back.

But then, oh dear, there were such lots of things that must be left behind.

There were those dear hills on which she had run about nearly every day and picked flowers; and they looked prettier than ever now, because the myrtle-bushes were just getting covered over with their pretty white flowers, which made all the hills look white.

And then there were those nice meadows where the stream of water ran, and where the hay had all been made.

And then the sea, the nice blue, rolling sea! Ah, how she would have liked to find a bottle big enough to hold it all, and carry it away to London!

But the hills, and the meadows, and the sea, must all be left behind.

And so must the funny long-legged sheep, and the chickens, and the two donkeys, Jack and Jenny, as well as a little calf which had been born since she came, and which knew Rosy quite well.

It made her cry when she went to say good-bye to all these pets.

She cried too when old Peter put his

hand on her head and blessed his little pet, and told her that he should never see her again in this world.

But they had to go; and the bustle of packing up again was, after all, 'very good fun.'

Those little legs went up and down stairs a great many times to fetch things for nurse, who was *so* busy; and besides there were lots of small parcels that no one else could carry but the little person to whom they belonged.

They had to be put into one little heap for fear that some of them should be forgotten.

Julia was left out this time to be a companion for Rosy, during the journey; and Julia was made to carry a splendid picture-book with stories about donkeys

and ... and ... and ... which **Rosy**
could now read pretty well, because she had
read them twice over, and she liked the
stories very much.

At last the carriage which was to take
them to the train came up to the door; and
the boxes were put up, and then mamma
got in, and then **Rosy** with as many little
parcels as she could carry.

Cecile brought her the others, and poor
Cecile's eyes were red with crying. She
did not like parting with her little **Rosy** at
all, for besides taking care of her when she
fell into the river, she had done kind things
for her every day because she had loved the
little one very much.

Rosy's papa and mamma had been very
kind to Cecile too; and now she had to go
and find another place; so she was very sad.

' Rosy will send you a beautiful cap with lots of ribbons.'

and dogs, and cats, and birds, which Rosy could now read pretty well, because she had read them twice over, and she liked the stories very much.

At last the carriage which was to take them to the train came up to the door; and the boxes were put up, and then mamma got in, and then Rosy with as many little parcels as she could carry.

Cecile brought her the others, and poor Cecile's eyes were red with crying. She did not like parting with her little Rosy at all, for besides taking care of her when she fell into the river, she had done kind things for her every day because she had loved the little one very much.

Rosy's papa and mamma had been very kind to Cecile too; and now she had to go and find another place; so she was very sad.

' Rosy will send you a beautiful cap with lots of ribbons.'

And when Rosy saw her red eyes it made her feel sad too; and she wished very much that Cecile were going with them. It seemed worse to leave her behind than it was to leave the hills, and fields, and sea, and all her pets.

So Rosy put her arms round Cecile's neck and said,—

' Don't cry, Cecy; Rosy loves you very much; she'll come back some day to see you. Rosy 'll send Cecile a beau'ful cap with lots of ribbons; good-bye, dear Cecile;' and she stroked her cheeks.

But the coachman was up on the box by this time, and nurse was up there too, and papa wanted to get in. So Cecile had to go back, and stand at the gate, and watch them drive off.

And the coachman cracked his whip;

and the horses began to trot, and their bells to tinkle.

Then Rosy's spirits rose again, and she waved her handkerchief out of the window and cried out,—

'Good-bye, Cecile; good-bye, everybody; we're all going back to England.'

LONDON:
Printed by STRANGEWAYS & WALDEN, Castle St. Leicester Sq.

NEW BOOKS FOR CHILDREN.

Price Half-a-crown each, with Engravings.

" A series of books for little people which does credit to its
publishers."— *Guardian*.

MY FIRST BOOK : Simple Readings for Very Little
People.   With 96 Illustrations.   Large Type.   Square 16mo. 2*s*. 6*d*.

MY FATHER'S HAND ; and other Stories for the
Young.   By Mrs. Carey Brock.   In 16mo.   Four Engravings, 2*s*. 6*d*.

GOOD DOGS : True Stories of our Four-footed Friends.
Large Type.   Eight Engravings, 2*s*. 6*d*.

WINGED THINGS : True Stories about Birds.   Large
Type.   Twelve Engravings, 2*s*. 6*d*.

GREAT THINGS DONE BY LITTLE PEOPLE.
Large Type.   Six Engravings, 2*s*. 6*d*.

THE DOVE AND OTHER STORIES OF OLD.
Large Type.   Eight Engravings by Harrison Weir, 2*s*. 6*d*.

New Books for Children.

THE LITTLE FOX: the Story of Captain M'Clintock's Arctic Expedition. Large Type. Four Engravings, 2s. 6d.

LITTLE ANIMALS DESCRIBED FOR LITTLE People. Large Type. Eight Engravings by Harrison Weir, 2s. 6d.

LITTLE FACTS FOR LITTLE PEOPLE. By the Author of "Waggie and Wattie." Large Type. Twelve Engravings, 2s. 6d.

TRUE STORIES FOR LITTLE PEOPLE. Large Type. Ten Engravings, 2s. 6d.

WAGGIE AND WATTIE; or, Nothing in Vain. By S. T. C. Four Engravings, 2s. 6d.

AGATHOS; and other Sunday Stories. By the Bishop of Oxford. Square 16mo. Twenty-sixth edition; Engravings, 2s. 6d.

SUNDAY AFTERNOONS IN THE NURSERY: Familiar Narratives from Genesis. Twenty Engravings, 2s. 6d.

CHILDREN OF LONG AGO. By the Author of " Words for Women." Twelve Engravings, 2s. 6d.

WORK FOR ALL; and other Tales. By C. E. B. Engravings. Third Edition, 2s. 6d.

THE YOUNG COTTAGER; Christmas Eve; and other Stories in Rhyme. Frontispiece and Engravings, 2s. 6d.

SEELEY, JACKSON, AND HALLIDAY, 54 FLEET STREET, LONDON.